ISBN 978-1-4803-0919-7

CORPORATION
7777 W. BLUEMOUND RD. P.O. BOX 13819 MILWAUKEE, WI 53213

Visit Hal Leonard Online at
www.halleonard.com

contents

4	The Air That I Breathe	*The Hollies*
10	American Pie	*Don McLean*
7	Annie's Song	*John Denver*
22	Another Brick in the Wall	*Pink Floyd*
24	At Seventeen	*Janis Ian*
28	Baby Don't Get Hooked on Me	*Mac Davis*
30	Baby, I Love Your Way	*Peter Frampton*
34	Baby, I'm-A Want You	*Bread*
37	Ben	*Michael Jackson*
40	Billy Don't Be a Hero	*Bo Donaldson & The Heywoods*
46	Brand New Key	*Melanie*
48	Cat's in the Cradle	*Harry Chapin*
43	Chevy Van	*Sammy Johns*
52	Copacabana (At the Copa)	*Barry Manilow*
58	Could It Be Magic	*Barry Manilow*
60	Cracklin' Rosie	*Neil Diamond*
55	Delta Dawn	*Helen Reddy*
66	Don't It Make My Brown Eyes Blue	*Crystal Gayle*
68	Dust in the Wind	*Kansas*
63	Escape (The Piña Colada Song)	*Rupert Holmes*
70	Everything Is Beautiful	*Ray Stevens*
76	Free Bird	*Lynyrd Skynyrd*
78	Garden Party	*Rick Nelson*
73	Grease	*Frankie Valli*
81	Green-Eyed Lady	*Sugarloaf*
84	Help Me Make It Through the Night	*Sammi Smith*
86	(Hey, Won't You Play) Another Somebody Done Somebody Wrong Song	*B.J. Thomas*
98	A Horse with No Name	*America*
92	How Can You Mend a Broken Heart	*Bee Gees*
94	How Deep Is Your Love	*Bee Gees*
96	I Believe in Music	*Gallery*
89	(I Never Promised You A) Rose Garden	*Lynn Anderson*
104	I Shot the Sheriff	*Eric Clapton*
106	I Think I Love You	*The Partridge Family*
110	I'd Like to Teach the World to Sing	*The New Seekers*
112	If	*Bread*
114	If You Could Read My Mind	*Gordon Lightfoot*
101	If You Don't Know Me by Now	*Harold Melvin & The Bluenotes*
117	Imagine	*John Lennon & Plastic Ono Band*
120	The Joker	*Steve Miller Band*

126	Just the Way You Are	*Billy Joel*
130	Lady Marmalade	*LaBelle*
134	Laughter in the Rain	*Neil Sedaka*
123	Lay Down Sally	*Eric Clapton*
145	Listen to the Music	*The Doobie Brothers*
136	The Long and Winding Road	*The Beatles*
138	Maggie May	*Rod Stewart*
140	Make It with You	*Bread*
142	Margaritaville	*Jimmy Buffett*
151	Maybe I'm Amazed	*Wings*
154	Me and You and a Dog Named Boo	*Lobo*
148	Moondance	*Van Morrison*
156	My Love	*Paul McCartney & Wings*
162	New World Coming	*Mama Cass Elliot*
164	Nights in White Satin	*The Moody Blues*
159	One Toke Over the Line	*Brewer & Shipley*
166	Peaceful Easy Feeling	*Eagles*
174	Please Come to Boston	*Dave Loggins*
178	Reunited	*Peaches & Herb*
184	Right Time of the Night	*Jennifer Warnes*
169	Rocky Mountain High	*John Denver*
181	She Believes in Me	*Kenny Rogers*
190	Silly Love Songs	*Wings*
196	Sister Golden Hair	*America*
202	Snowbird	*Anne Murray*
204	Sundown	*Gordon Lightfoot*
206	Sweet Home Alabama	*Lynyrd Skynyrd*
187	Teach Your Children	*Crosby, Stills, Nash & Young*
199	Three Times a Lady	*Commodores*
208	We've Only Just Begun	*Carpenters*
210	When I Need You	*Leo Sayer*
215	Why Don't We Get Drunk	*Jimmy Buffett*
212	The Wreck of the Edmund Fitzgerald	*Gordon Lightfoot*
218	Yesterday Once More	*Carpenters*
221	Y.M.C.A.	*Village People*
224	You Are So Beautiful	*Joe Cocker*
226	You Make Me Feel Like Dancing	*Leo Sayer*
236	You Needed Me	*Anne Murray*
229	You've Got a Friend	*James Taylor*
232	Your Mama Don't Dance	*Loggins & Messina*

The Air That I Breathe

Words and Music by Albert Hammond and Michael Hazlewood

First note

Verse
Moderately

1. If   I could make a wish, _____   I
2. No   cig - a - rettes, no sleep, _____   no

think   I'd pass; _____   can't   think of
light,   no sound, _____   noth - ing to

1.
an - y - thing _____ I need. _____
eat, no books _____ to read. _____

Bridge

2.

Mak - ing love with you _____ has left me

peace - ful, warm and tired. _____ What _____ more could I

ask? _____ There's noth - ing left to be de - sired. _____

Verse

3. Peace came up - on me and it leaves me weak. _____

_____ Sleep, si - lent

To Coda ⊕

an - gel, go _____ to sleep.

Chorus

Some - times _____ all I need is the air _____

that I breathe ___ and to love you. ___

All I need is the air ___ that I breathe, ___ yes, to

love you. ___ All I need is the air ___

___ that I breathe. ___ Ah, ah, ___

ah, ah, ___ ah, ah, ___ ah.

D.S. al Coda

Coda

ah.

sleep.

Annie's Song

Words and Music by John Denver

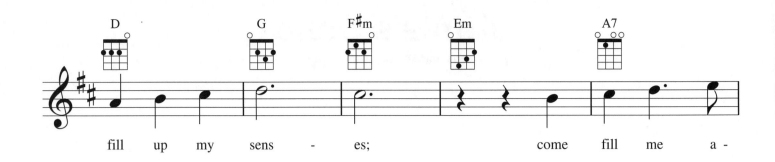

fill up my sens - es; come fill me a -

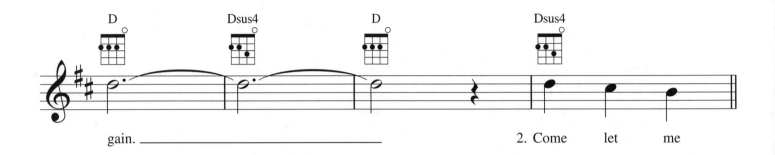

gain. _____ 2. Come let me

Verse

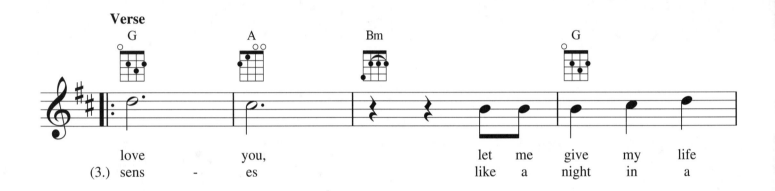

love you,
(3.) sens - es let me give my life like a night in a

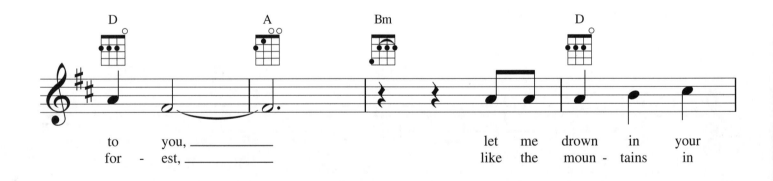

to you, _____ let me drown in your
for - est, _____ like the moun - tains in

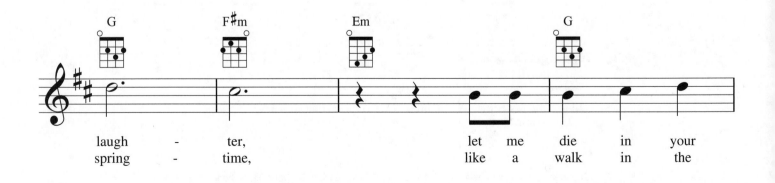

laugh - ter, let me die in your
spring - time, like a walk in the

arms. _____ Let me lay down be - side

rain. _____ Like a storm in the des -

you, let me al - ways be with you. _____

ert, like a sleep - y blue o - cean, _____

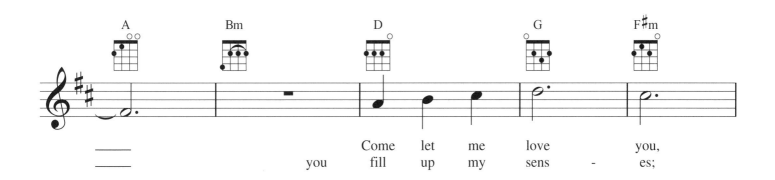

_____ Come let me love you,

_____ you come fill up my sens - es;

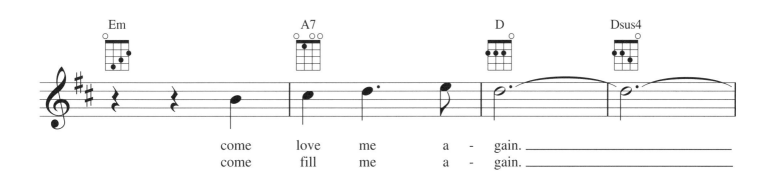

come love me a - gain. _____

come fill me a - gain. _____

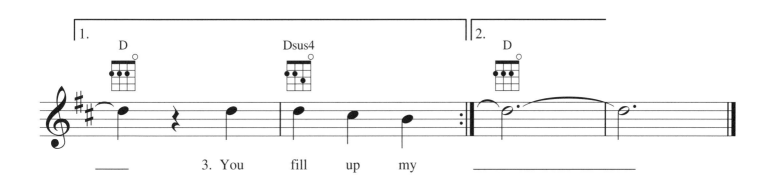

_____ 3. You fill up my _____

American Pie

Words and Music by Don McLean

First note

Intro
Freely

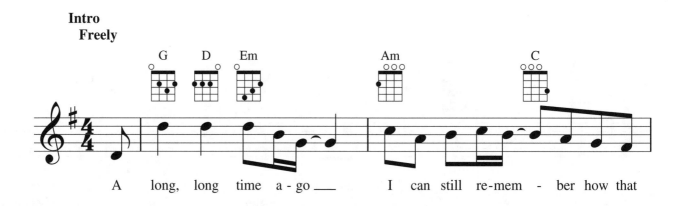

A long, long time a-go ___ I can still re-mem - ber how that

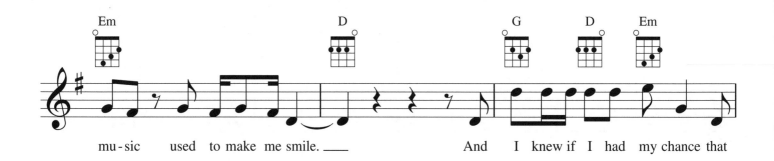

mu - sic used to make me smile. ___ And I knew if I had my chance that

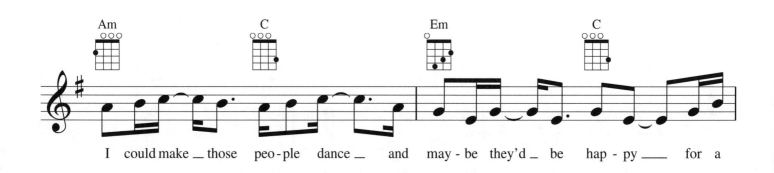

I could make ___ those peo-ple dance ___ and may - be they'd ___ be hap - py ___ for a

while. But Feb - ru - ar - y made me shiv - er,

with ev - 'ry pa - per I'd de - liv - er. Bad news on the door - step, I

could - n't take one more step. I can't re-mem-ber if I cried ____ when I

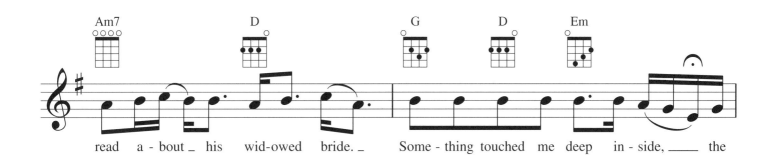

read a - bout _ his wid-owed bride. _ Some - thing touched me deep in - side, _____ the

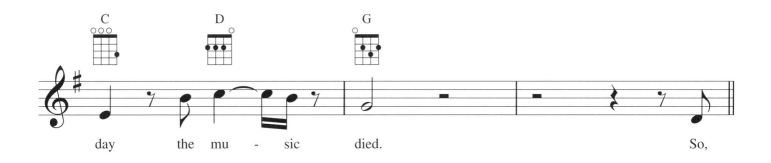

day the mu - sic died. So,

Chorus
Moderately

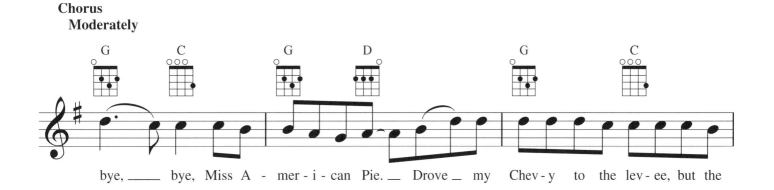

bye, _____ bye, Miss A - mer - i - can Pie. _ Drove _ my Chev - y to the lev - ee, but the

11

lev - ee was dry. ___ An' them good ol' ___ boys ___ were drink - in'

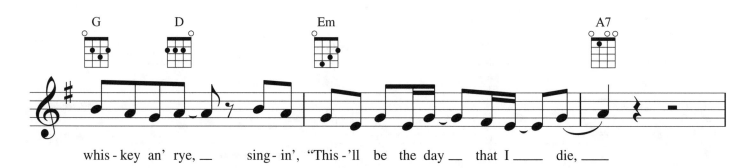

whis - key an' rye, ___ sing - in', "This -'ll be the day ___ that I ___ die, ___

Faster

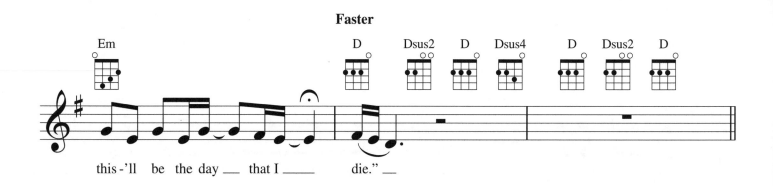

this -'ll be the day ___ that I ___ die." ___

Verse

1. Did you ___ write the book of love ___ and do you ___ have faith in
(2.) ten years ___ we've been on our own, ___ an' moss ___ grows fat on

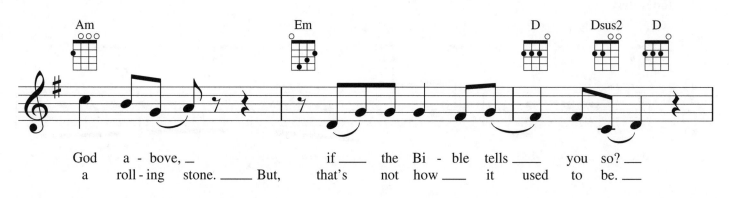

God a - bove, ___ if ___ the Bi - ble tells ___ you so? ___
a roll - ing stone. ___ But, that's not how ___ it used to be. ___

Now, __ do you _____ be - lieve __ in rock 'n' roll? ___ Can
When the jest - er sang for the king an' queen _____ in a

mu - sic save your ___ mor - tal soul? An' __ can you teach me __
coat he bor - rowed from ___ James Dean. An' a voice __ that came __

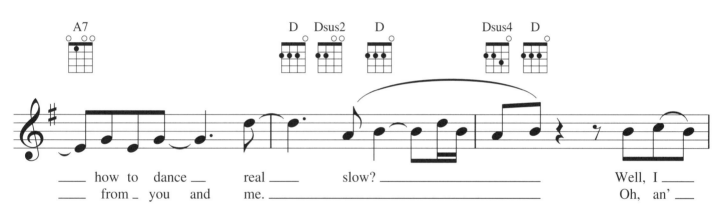

___ how to dance __ real ____ slow? _____ Well, I ____
___ from _ you and me. _____ Oh, an' __

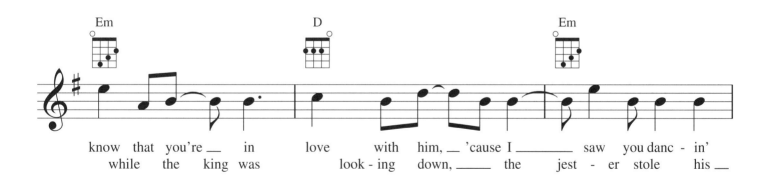

know that you're __ in love with him, __ 'cause I _____ saw you danc - in'
while the king was look - ing down, _____ the jest - er stole his __

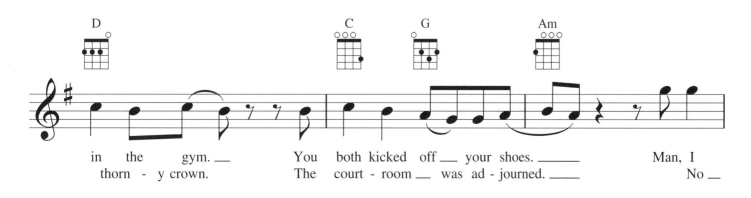

in the gym. __ You both kicked off __ your shoes. _____ Man, I
thorn - y crown. The court - room __ was ad - journed. ____ No __

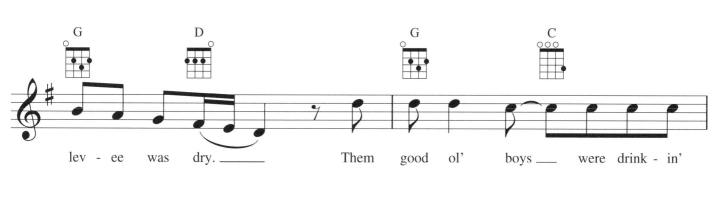

lev - ee was dry. _____ Them good ol' boys _____ were drink - in'

whis - key an' rye, _ an' sing - in' this -'ll be the day _ that I _____ die,

1.

this -'ll be the day _ that I _____ die." _ 2. Now, _ for

2.

Verse

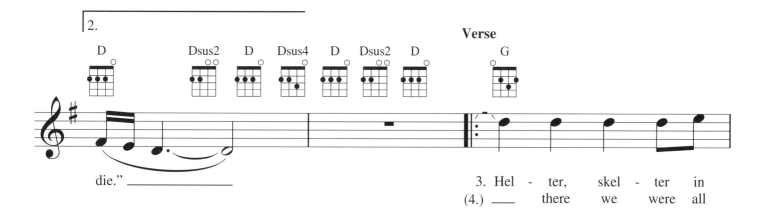

die." _____

3. Hel - ter, skel - ter in
(4.) _ there we were all

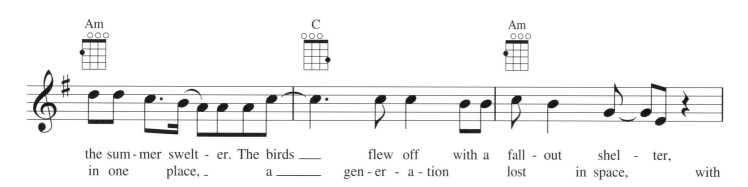

the sum - mer swelt - er. The birds _ flew off with a fall - out shel - ter,
in one place, _ a _ gen - er - a - tion lost in space, with

march - in' tune. ___   We all ___ got up to dance, _____ oh, _____ but
fists of rage.   No an - gel born in Hell _____ could

we nev - er got ___ the chance. ___   'Cause _ the play - ers tried _ to take _
break that Sa - tan's spell. _____   And as the flames ___ climbed high in -

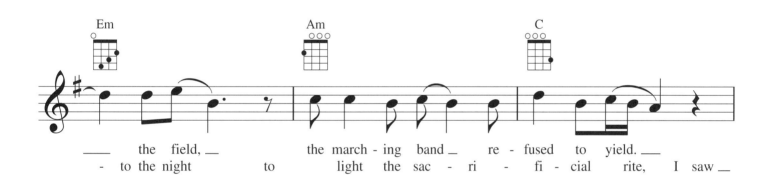

___ the field, _   the march - ing band _ re - fused to yield. ___
- to the night   to   light the sac - ri - fi - cial rite, I saw _

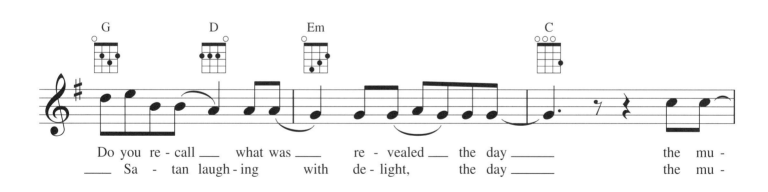

Do you re - call ___ what was ___ re - vealed ___ the day ___   the mu -
___ Sa - tan laugh - ing with de - light, the day ___   the mu -

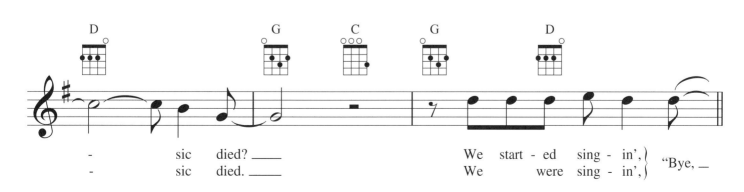

- sic died? ___   We start - ed sing - in', } "Bye, _
- sic died. ___   We were sing - in', }

Chorus

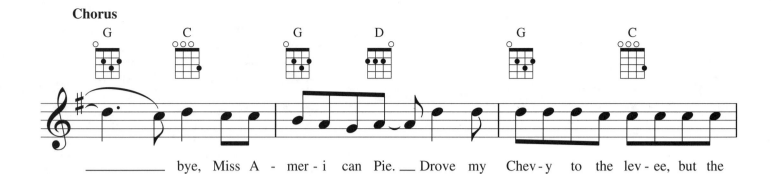

_____ bye, Miss A - mer - i can Pie. __ Drove my Chev-y to the lev- ee, but the

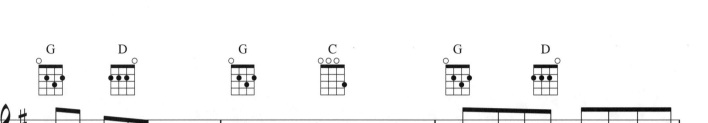

lev - ee was dry. __ Them good ol' boys __ were drink- in' whis - key and rye, __ an' sing - in'

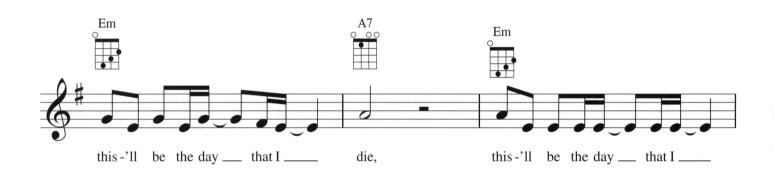

this -'ll be the day __ that I ____ die, this -'ll be the day __ that I ____

die." __ 4. Oh, _____ an' _ die." _____

Verse
Freely

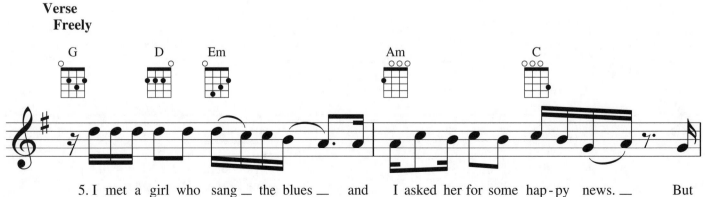

5. I met a girl who sang __ the blues __ and I asked her for some hap-py news. __ But

18

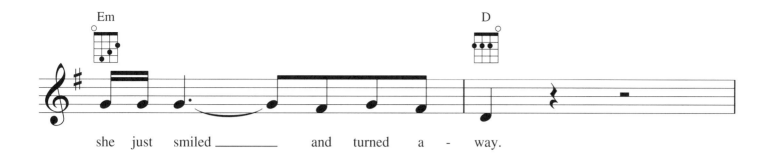

she just smiled _____ and turned a - way.

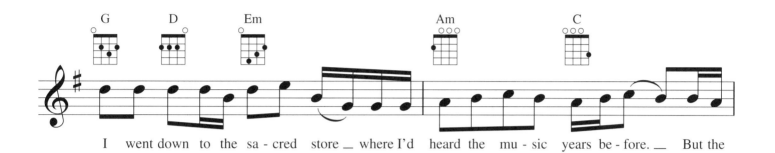

I went down to the sa - cred store _ where I'd heard the mu - sic years be - fore. _ But the

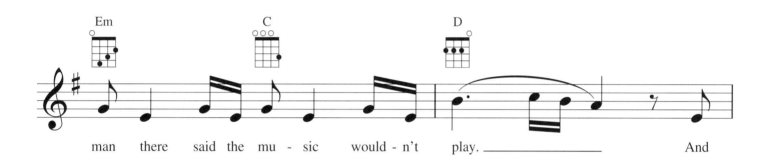

man there said the mu - sic would - n't play. _____ And

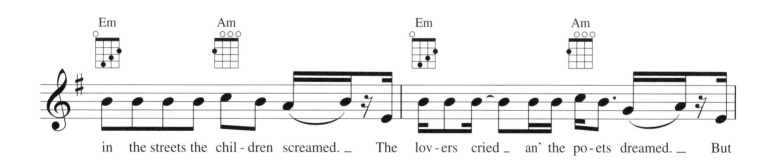

in the streets the chil - dren screamed. _ The lov - ers cried _ an' the po - ets dreamed. _ But

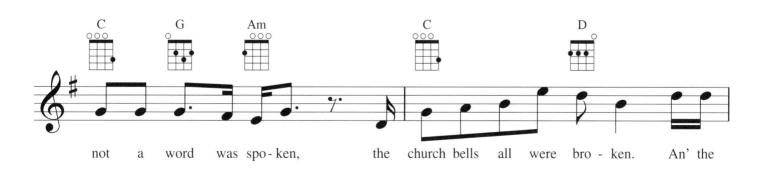

not a word was spo - ken, the church bells all were bro - ken. An' the

Outro-Chorus

Another Brick in the Wall

Words and Music by Roger Waters

First note

Verse
Moderate groove

1., 2. We don't need _ no ed - u - ca - tion.

We don't need _ no thought con - trol, _

no dark sar - cas - m

in the class - room.

G

Teach - er, leave __ them kids a - lone. __
Teach - er, leave __ us kids a - lone. __

Dm

Hey, teach - er! Leave them kids a - lone! ___
Hey, teach - er! Leave us kids a - lone! ___

Chorus

Am G F C

All in all, __ it's just an - oth - er brick in the
All in all, __ you're just an - oth - er brick in the

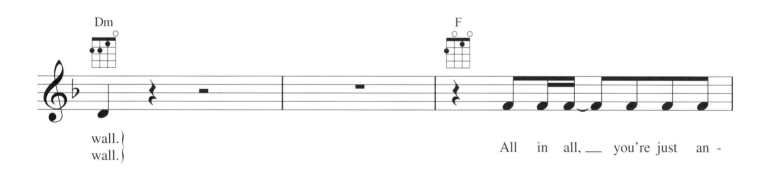

Dm F

wall.)
wall.)

All in all, __ you're just an -

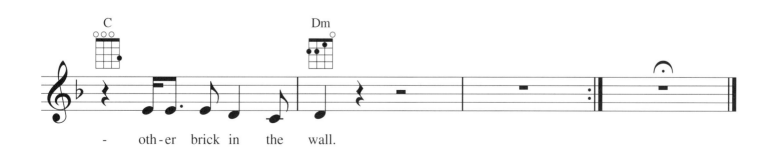

C Dm

- oth - er brick in the wall.

At Seventeen

Words and Music by Janis Ian

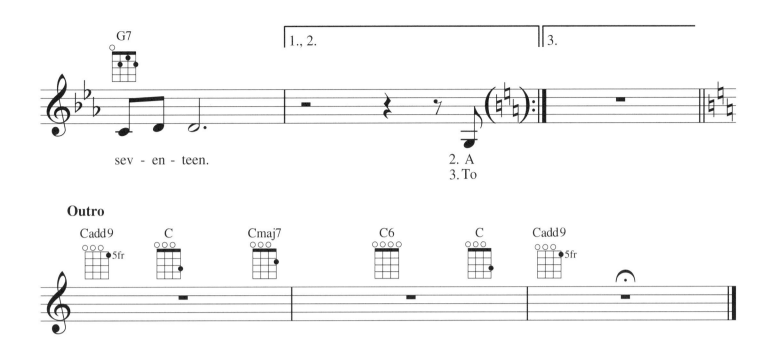

sev - en - teen.

2. A
3. To

Outro

Additional Lyrics

2. A brown-eyed girl in hand-me-downs whose name I never could pronounce,
    Said, "Pity, please, the ones who serve; they only get what they deserve.
    And the rich, relationed hometown queen marries into what she needs,
    With a guarantee of company and haven for the elderly.

Chorus: "Remember those who win the game, lose the love they sought to gain
    In debentures of quality and dubious integrity.
    Their small-town eyes will gape at you in dull surprise when payment due
    Exceeds accounts received, at seventeen."

3. To those of us who knew the pain of valentines that never came,
    And those whose names were never called when choosing sides for basketball,
    It was long ago and far away; the world was younger than today,
    And dreams were all they gave for free to ugly duckling girls like me.

Chorus: We all play the game and when we dare to cheat ourselves at solitaire,
    Inventing lovers on the phone, repenting other lives unknown
    That call and say, "Come dance with me," and murmur vague obscenities
    At ugly girls like me, at seventeen.

Baby Don't Get Hooked on Me

Words and Music by Mac Davis

1. Girl, you're get- tin' that look in your eyes; ___
2. Girl, you're a hot- blood- ed wom- an, child, ___

and it's start- ing to wor - ry me.
and it's warm where you're touch - ing me.

I ain't read - y for no fam- i- ly ties; ___
But I can tell by your trem- bl- in' smile, ___

no- bod- y's gon- na hur- ry me.
you're see- ing way too much in me.

Pre-Chorus

Just keep it friend- ly, girl, ___ 'cause I ___ don't want to leave. ___
Girl, don't let your life ___ get tan- gled up with mine, ___

Baby, I Love Your Way

Words and Music by Peter Frampton

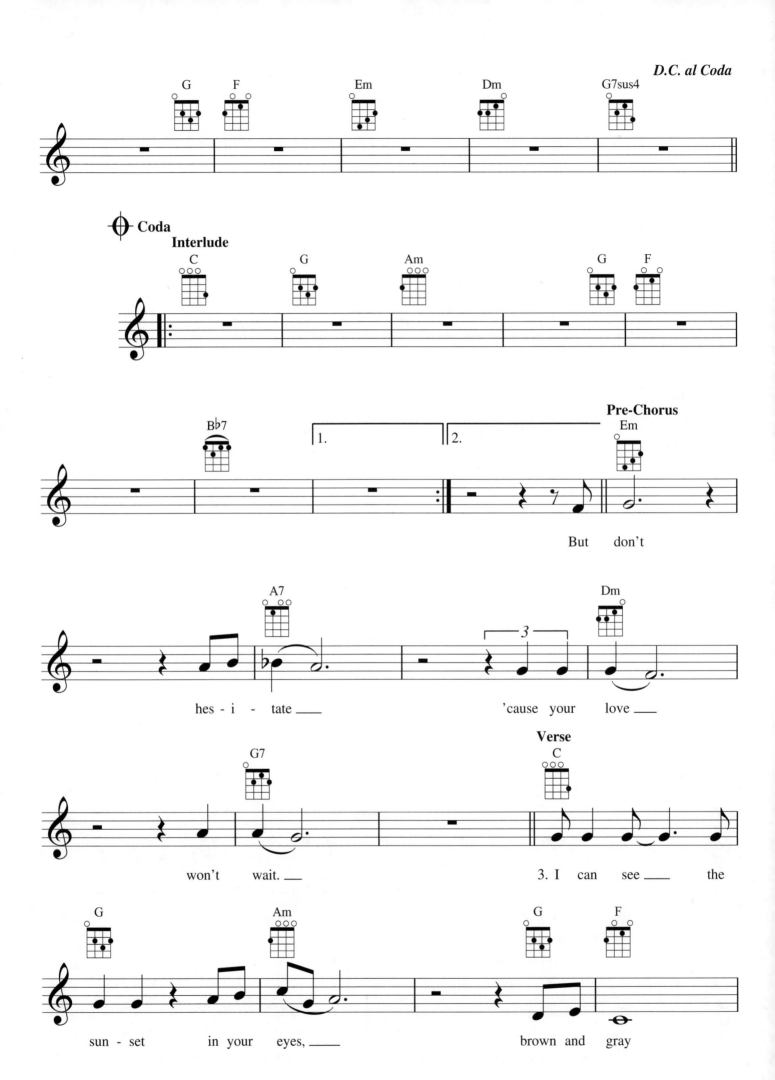

and blue be-sides. Clouds are stalk-ing

is-lands in the sun. ____ I wish I could

buy one out of sea-son. But

Pre-Chorus

don't hes-i-tate ____ 'cause your

love _____ won't wait. _____

Outro-Chorus   *Repeat and fade*

Ooh, ba-by, I love ___ your way. _____
Wan-na tell you I love ___ your way. _____
Wan-na be with you night ___ and day. _____

Baby, I'm-a Want You

Words and Music by David Gates

Ben

Words by Don Black
Music by Walter Scharf

Billy Don't Be a Hero

Words and Music by Peter Callander and Mitch Murray

Verse

3. I heard his fi - an - cée _____ got a let - ter
that told how Bil - ly died _____ that day. _____ The let - ter said that he _____
_____ was a he - ro; she should be proud he died _____ that way. _____
I heard she threw the let - ter a - way. _____

Outro

(Instrumental)

Repeat and fade

Chevy Van

Words and Music by Sammy Johns

Brand New Key

Words and Music by Melanie Safka

First note

Verse
Moderately bright, in 2

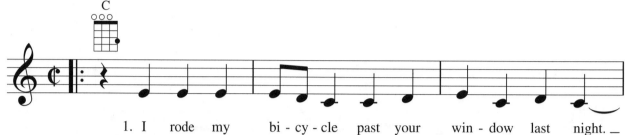

1. I rode my bi - cy - cle past your win - dow last night.
2., 3. *See additional lyrics*

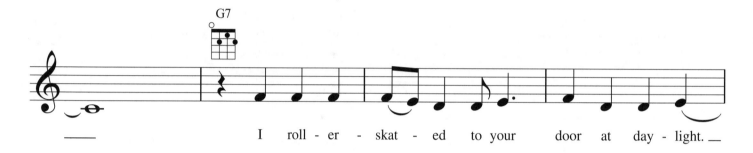

I roll - er - skat - ed to your door at day - light.

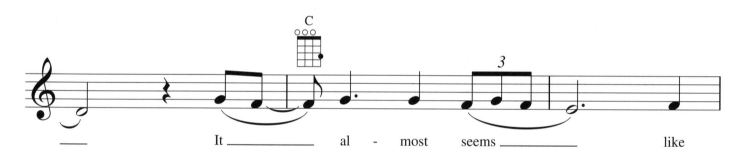

It ____ al - most seems ____ like

you're a - void - ing me. ____ I'm o - kay a - lone, ____

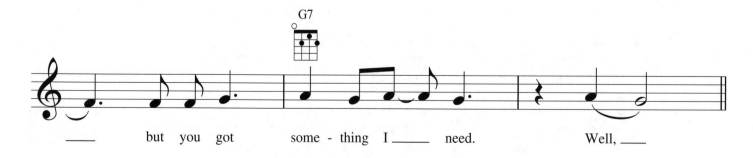

____ but you got some - thing I ____ need. Well, ____

Chorus

C

I got a brand - new pair of roll - er skates, you got a brand - new

C

key. I think that we should get to - geth - er and

G7   C   F

try them out, ___ you see. _____ I been look - ing a - round ___ a while;

G7   C

you got some - thing for me. Oh, I got a brand - new pair of roll - er skates,

G7   1., 2.   C   3.   C

you got a brand - new key. key.

Additional Lyrics

2. I ride my bike, I roller skate, don't drive no car.
   Don't go too fast, but I go pretty far.
   For somebody who don't drive, I been all around the world.
   Some people think I done all right for a girl.

3. I asked your mother if you were at home.
   She said yes, but you weren't alone.
   Well, sometimes I think that you're avoiding me.
   I'm okay alone, but you got something I need.

Cat's in the Cradle

Words and Music by Harry Chapin and Sandy Chapin

First note

Verse
Moderate Folk style, in 2

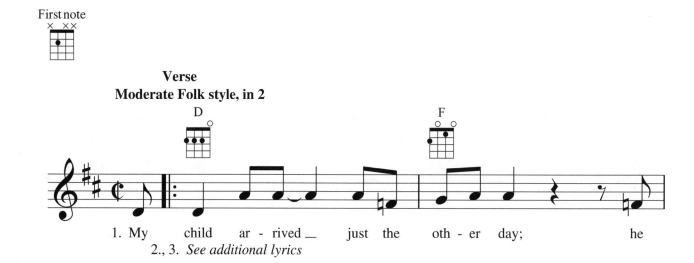

1. My child ar-rived __ just the oth-er day; he
2., 3. *See additional lyrics*

came to the world in the u-su-al way. __ But there were planes to catch __ and

bills to pay; __ he learned to walk while I was a-way. And he was

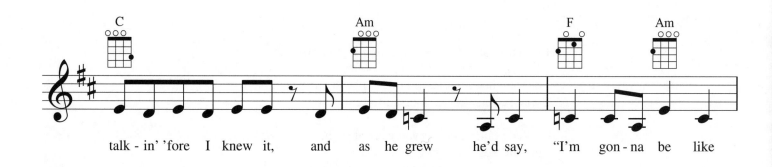

talk-in' 'fore I knew it, and as he grew he'd say, "I'm gon-na be like

Outro-Chorus

curred to me: ___ he'd grown up just like me. My

boy was just like me. And the cat's in the cra-dle and the

sil - ver spoon, ___ lit - tle boy blue and the man ___ in the moon. ___

"When you com - in' home, Son?" "I don't know when, but we'll get to-geth-er then, ___

rit.

___ Dad. ___ We're gon - na have a good time then."

Additional Lyrics

2. My son turned ten just the other day;
   He said, "Thanks for the ball, Dad. Come on, let's play.
   Can you teach me to throw?"
   I said, "Not today, I got a lot to do."
   He said, "That's okay." And he, he walked away,
   But his smile never dimmed, it said,
   "I'm gonna be like him, yeah.
   You know I'm gonna be like him."

3. Well, he came from college just the other day;
   So much like a man I just had to say,
   "Son, I'm proud of you. Can you sit for a while?"
   He shook his head and he said with a smile,
   "What I'd really like, Dad, is to borrow the car keys.
   See you later; can I have them, please?"

Copacabana
(At the Copa)

Music by Barry Manilow
Lyric by Bruce Sussman and Jack Feldman

young and they had each oth - er; who could ask for more? At the

Chorus

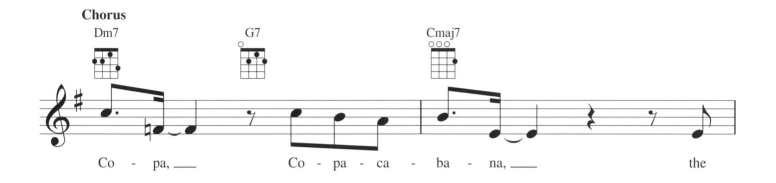

Co - pa, ___ Co - pa - ca - ba - na, ___ the

hot - test ___ spot north of ___ Ha - va - na. ___ At the

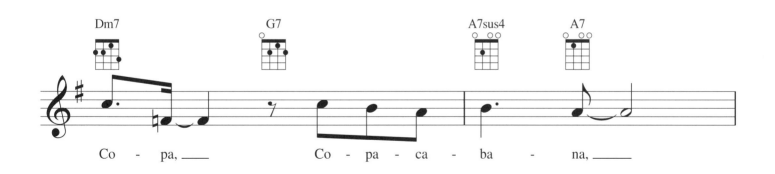

Co - pa, ___ Co - pa - ca - ba - na, ___

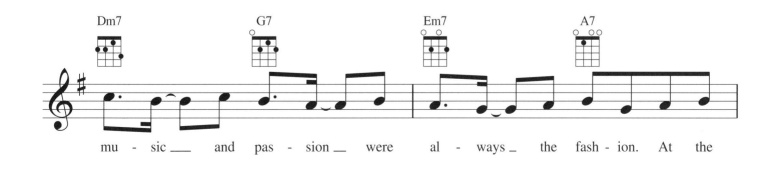

mu - sic ___ and pas - sion ___ were al - ways ___ the fash - ion. At the

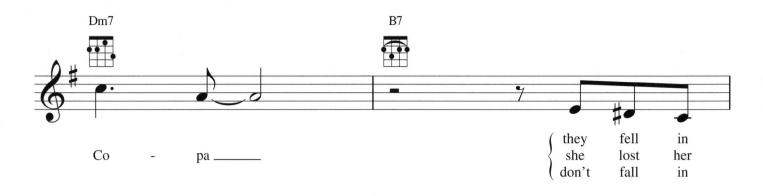

they fell in
she lost her
don't fall in

(Co - pa, ___   Co - pa - ca - ba - na.) ___
love.
love.
love.

2. His name was

Additional Lyrics

2. His name was Rico; he wore a diamond,
   He was escorted to his chair, he saw Lola dancing there.
   And when she finished, he called her over,
   But Rico went a bit too far; Tony sailed across the bar.
   And then the punches flew and chairs were smashed in two.
   There was blood and a single gunshot, but just who shot who?

3. Her name is Lola; she was a showgirl,
   But that was thirty years ago when they used to have a show.
   Now it's a disco, but not for Lola.
   Still in the dress she used to wear, faded feathers in her hair.
   She sits there so refined and drinks herself half-blind.
   She lost her youth and she lost her Tony; now she's lost her mind.

Delta Dawn

Words and Music by Alex Harvey and Larry Collins

First note

Chorus
Moderately, in 2

Del - ta ___ Dawn, what's that flow - er you have on? ___

___ Could it be ___ a fad - ed rose ___ from days gone by?

And did I hear you say ___ he was a - meet - in' you here to - day ___

___ to take you to his man - sion ___ in the sky? ___

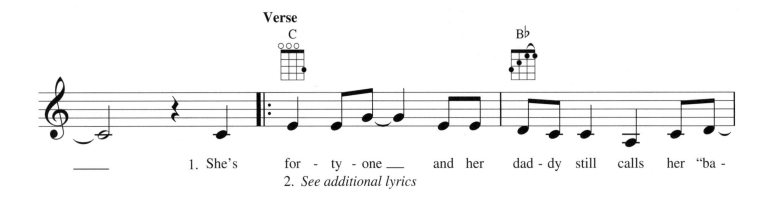

Verse

1. She's for - ty - one ___ and her dad - dy still calls her "ba -
2. *See additional lyrics*

- by." All the folks ___ 'round Browns - ville say she's

cra - zy 'cause she walks down - town with a suit - case in her

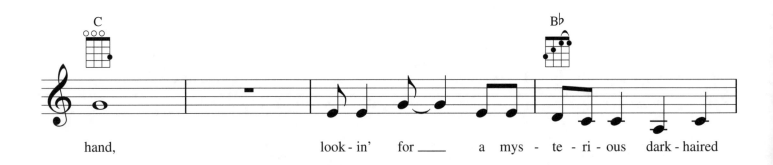

hand, look - in' for ___ a mys - te - ri - ous dark - haired

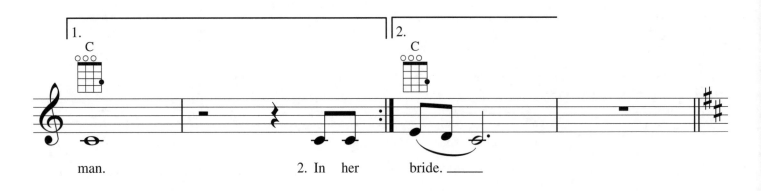

1.
man.

2.
2. In her bride. ___

Outro-Chorus

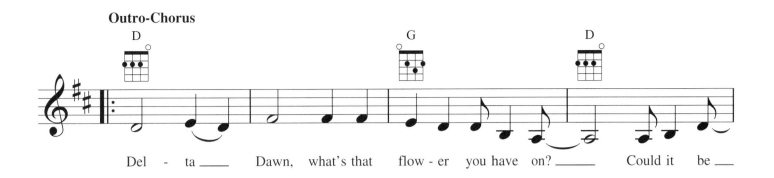

Del - ta _____ Dawn, what's that flow - er you have on? _____ Could it be _____

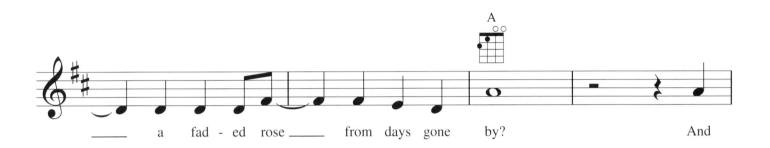

_____ a fad - ed rose _____ from days gone by? And

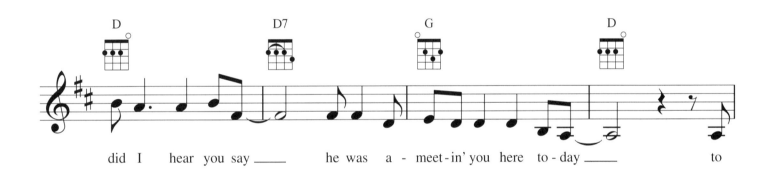

did I hear you say _____ he was a - meet-in' you here to - day _____ to

Repeat and fade

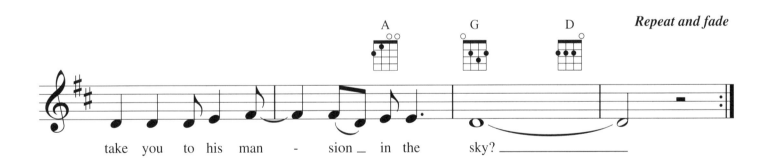

take you to his man - sion _ in the sky? _____

Additional Lyrics

2. In her younger days they called her Delta Dawn;
   Prettiest woman you ever laid eyes on.
   Then a man of low degree stood by her side,
   And he promised her he'd take her for his bride.

Could It Be Magic

Inspired by "Prelude in C Minor" by F. CHOPIN
Words and Music by Barry Manilow and Adrienne Anderson

Chorus

Come, come, come in - to ____ my

(D.S.) *Instrumental*

arms. Let me know ____ the won - der of

all of you. ____ Ba - by, I want ____ you now, ____ now,

now and hold ____ on fast. Could this be the mag -

To Coda ⊕

1.

- ic at last? _____

2.   *D.S. al Coda*   ⊕ **Coda**

Could it be mag - ic?

Cracklin' Rosie

Words and Music by Neil Diamond

First note

Verse
Moderately

1. Crack-lin' Ros-ie, get on board. __ We're gon-na ride __ till there ain't __
(D.C.) *Vocal ad lib.*

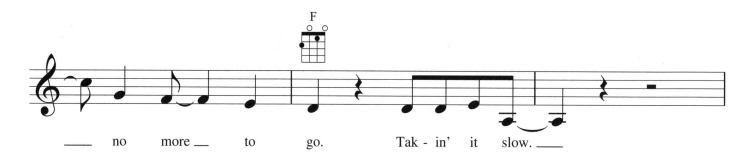

__ no more __ to go. Tak- in' it slow. __

And, Lord, don't you know I'll have me a time __ with a poor __

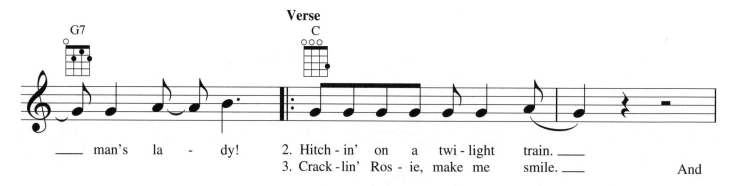

__ man's la - dy! 2. Hitch - in' on a twi - light train. __
3. Crack -lin' Ros - ie, make me smile. __ And

Ain't noth-ing here __ that I care __ to take __ a - long, may-be a song __
girl, if it lasts __ for a hour, __ that's __ al - right, 'cause we got all night __

to sing when I want. ___   Don't
to set the world right. ___

Dm   **G7**

need   to   say   please ___ to   no   man _____ for   a   hap - py
Find   us   a   dream ___ that   don't   ask _____ no   ques - tions,

Chorus

C   **C**   **F**

tune. _____ ⎱
yeah! _____ ⎰   Oh,   I   love   my ___

G   **C**   **F**   **G**   **C**

___ Ros - ie child. _   You   got   the   way   to   make ___ me   hap - py.

F   **G**   **C**   **Dm**

You   and   me,   we   go _____ in   style. ___   Crack - l - in' Rose, _ you're a store -

- bought wom-an,   but   you make me sing _ like a gui - tar hum - min'.   So

hang on to me, ___ girl, our song ___ keeps run - nin' on. _____

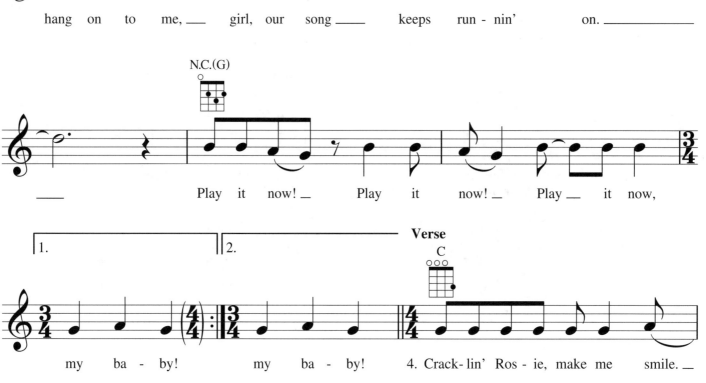

___ Play it now! _ Play it now! _ Play _ it now,

my ba - by! my ba - by! 4. Crack - lin' Ros - ie, make me smile. _

And, girl, if it lasts ___ for an hour, _____ that's al -

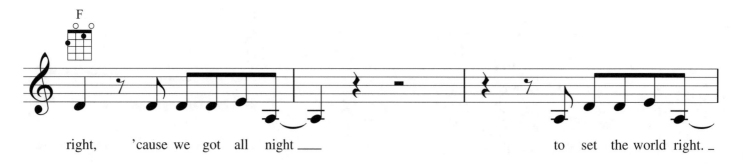

right, 'cause we got all night ___ to set the world right. _

D.C. and fade

Find us a dream ___ that don't ask _____ no ques - tions.

Escape

(The Piña Colada Song)

Words and Music by Rupert Holmes

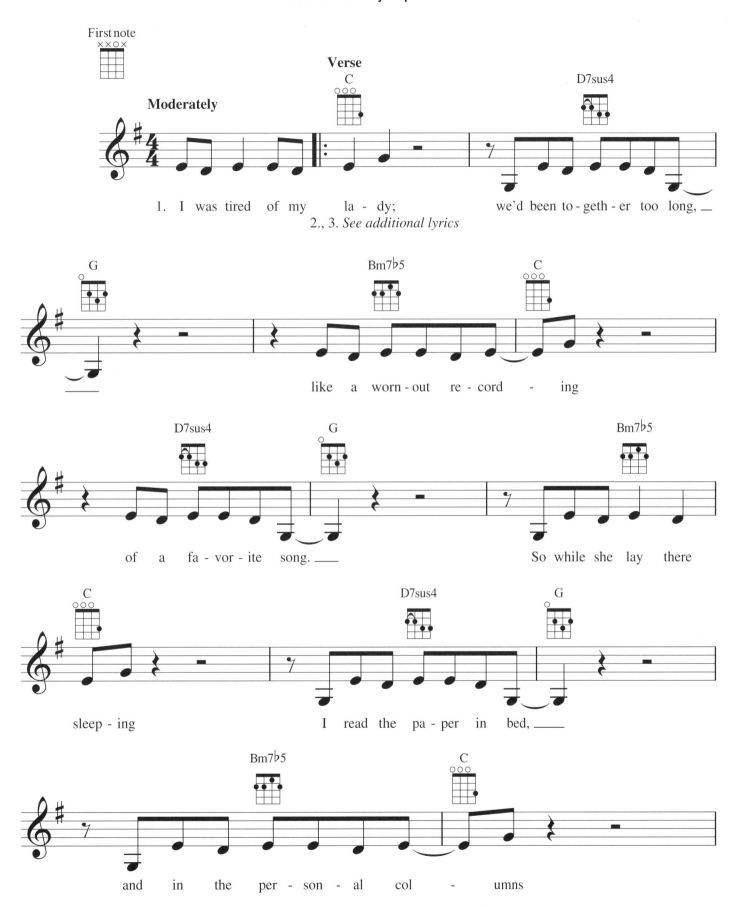

there was this let-ter I read: ___ "If you like pi - ña co -

Chorus

la - das   and get - ting caught in the rain,

if you're not in - to yo - ga,   if you have half a

brain,   if you'd like mak - ing love at

mid - night ___   in the dunes on the Cape,

then I'm the love that you've looked for.

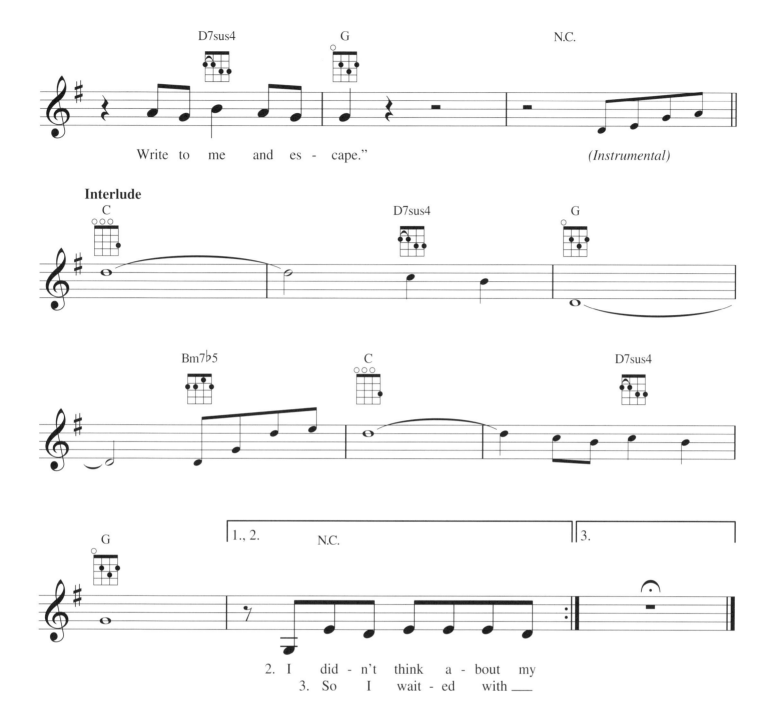

Write to me and es - cape." *(Instrumental)*

Interlude

2. I did - n't think a - bout my
3. So I wait - ed with ___

Additional Lyrics

2. I didn't think about my lady; I know that sounds kinda mean.
But me and my old lady have fallen into the same old dull routine.
So I wrote to the paper, took out a personal ad.
And though I'm nobody's poet, I thought it wasn't half bad:
"Yes, I like piña coladas and getting caught in the rain.
I'm not much into health food; I am into champagne.
I've got to meet you by tomorrow noon and cut through all this red tape,
At a bar called O'Malley's, where we'll plan our escape."

3. So I waited with high hopes, and she walked in the place.
I knew her smile in an instant, I knew the curve of her face.
It was my own lovely lady, and she said, "Oh, it's you!"
Then we laughed for a moment, and I said, "I never knew
That you like piña coladas and getting caught in the rain,
And the feel of the ocean and the taste of champagne.
If you'd like making love at midnight in the dunes on the Cape,
You're the lady I've looked for. Come with me and escape."

Don't It Make My Brown Eyes Blue

Words and Music by Richard Leigh

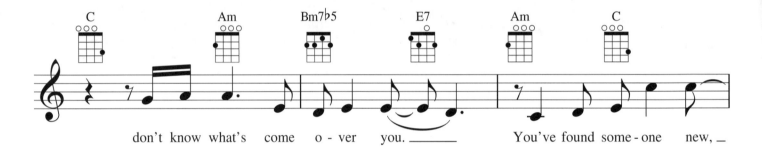

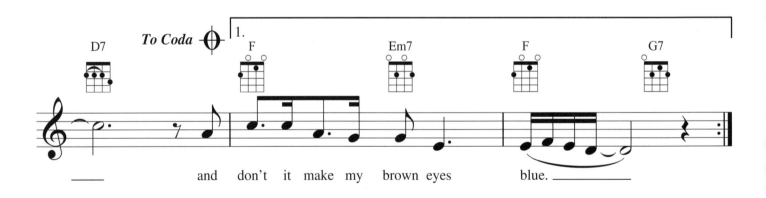

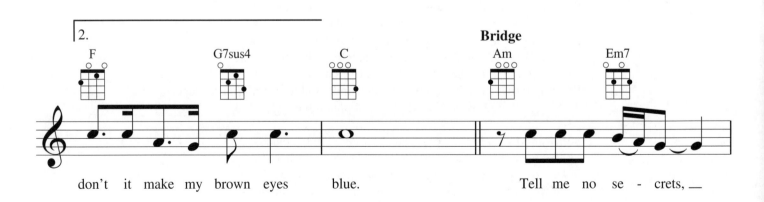

Additional Lyrics

2. I'll be fine when you're gone,
   I'll just cry all night long.
   Say it isn't true,
   And don't it make my brown eyes blue.

3. I didn't mean to treat you bad,
   Didn't know just what I had.
   But, honey, now I do,
   And don't it make my brown eyes,
   Don't it make my brown eyes,
   Don't it make my brown eyes blue.

Dust in the Wind

Words and Music by Kerry Livgren

Everything Is Beautiful

Words and Music by Ray Stevens

Additional Lyrics

2. We shouldn't care about the length of his hair or the color of his skin.
Don't worry about what shows from without but the love that lies within.
We gonna get it all together now and everything's gonna work out fine.
Just take a little time to look on the good side, my friend, and straighten it out in your mind.

Grease

Words and Music by Barry Gibb

First note

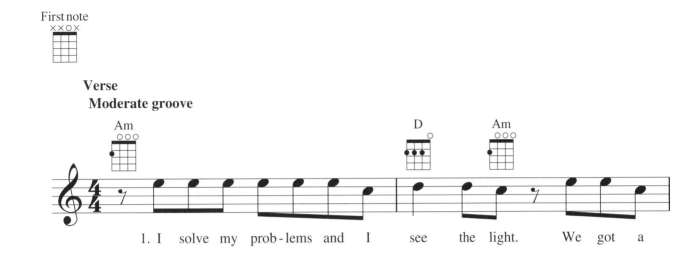

Verse
Moderate groove

1. I solve my prob-lems and I see the light. We got a

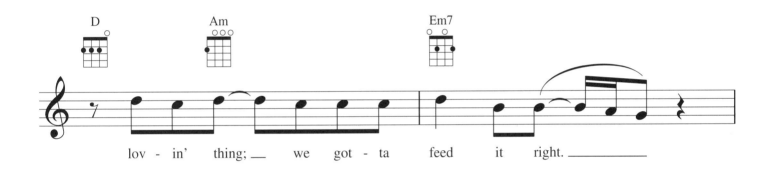

lov - in' thing; ___ we got - ta feed it right. ___

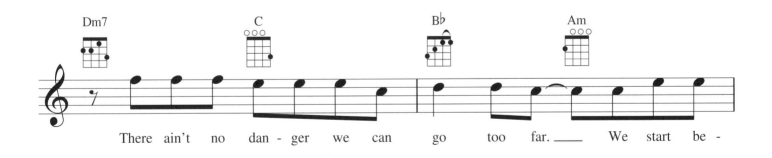

There ain't no dan - ger we can go too far. ___ We start be -

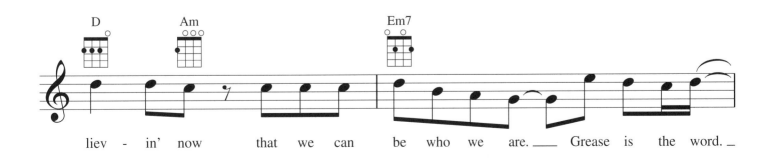

liev - in' now that we can be who we are. ___ Grease is the word. ___

Verse

2. They think our love is just a
3., 4. We take the pres - sure and we

grow - in' pain.   Why don't they   un - der - stand? ___ It's just a
throw a - way;   con - ven - tion - al - i - ty ___ be - longs to

cry - in' shame. _____   Their lips are ly - ing; on - ly
yes - ter - day. _____   There is a chance that we can

real is real. ___ We stop the fight right now; we got to
make it so far. ___ We start be - liev - ing now that we can

Chorus

be what we feel. ___ } Grease is the word. _____
be who we are. ___ }

It's got a groove, ___ it's got a mean - ing. ___

74

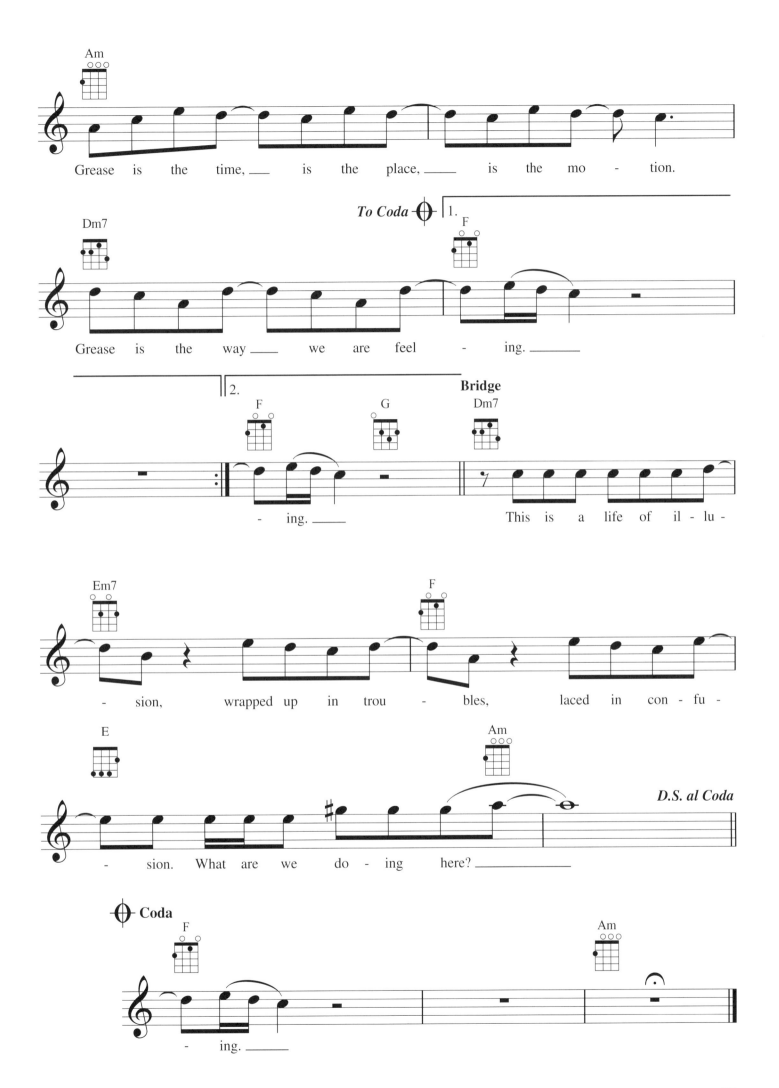

Free Bird

Words and Music by Allen Collins and Ronnie Van Zant

1. If I leave ___ here to - mor - row,
2. Bye, bye, ba - by; it's been a sweet love,

would you still re - mem - ber me?
though this feel - ing I can't change.

For I must be _____ trav - 'ling on now,
But please don't take it so bad - ly,

'cause there's too man - y plac - es I've ___ got to see. _____ }
'cause the Lord knows I'm to blame. ___ }

Chorus

But if I stayed ___ here with you, girl,

Garden Party

Words and Music by Rick Nelson

they all knew my name, _____ but

no one rec - og - nized _____ me;

I did - n't look the same. _____ But it's

Chorus

all right now, _____ I learned my les - son well. _

_____ You see, you can't please

To Coda

ev - 'ry - one, _ so you got to please your - self. _____

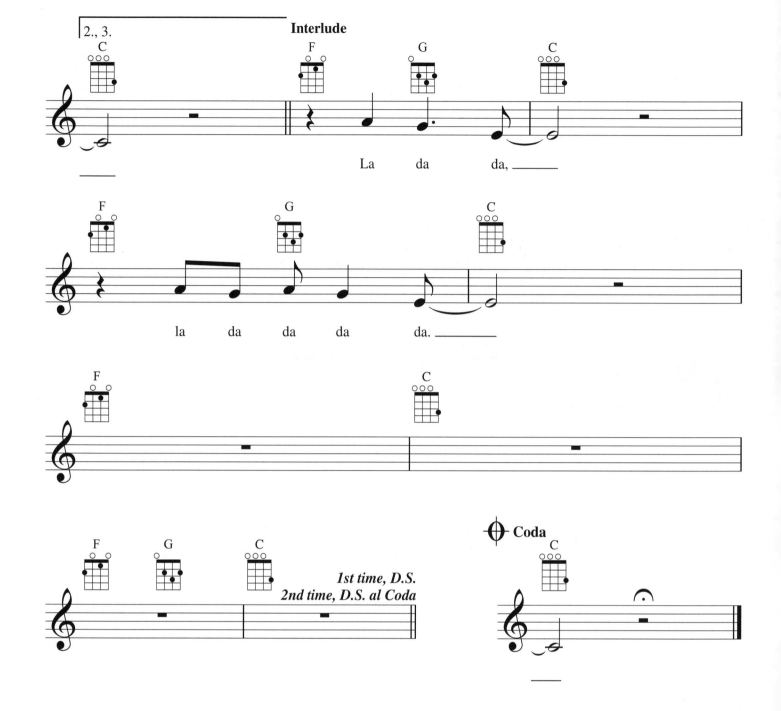

Additional Lyrics

2. People came for miles around; everyone was there.
   Yoko brought her walrus; there was magic in the air.
   And over in the corner, much to my surprise,
   Mr. Hughes hid in Dylan's shoes, wearing his disguise.

3. I played them all the old songs; I thought that's why they came.
   No one heard the music; we didn't look the same.
   I said hello to Mary Lou; she belongs to me.
   When I sang a song about a honky-tonk, it was time to leave.

4. Someone opened up a closet door and out stepped Johnny B. Goode,
   Playing guitar like a-ringin' a bell, and lookin' like he should.
   If you gotta play at garden parties, I wish you a lotta luck;
   But if memories were all I sang, I'd rather drive a truck.

Green-Eyed Lady

Words and Music by Jerry Corbetta, J.C. Phillips and David Riordan

First note

Intro
Bright, Psychedelic Rock

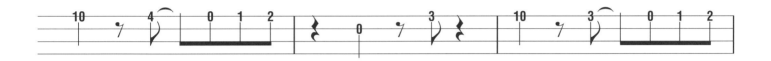

Verse

1. Green - eyed la - dy, love - ly la - dy
2. Green - eyed la - dy, wind - swept la - dy

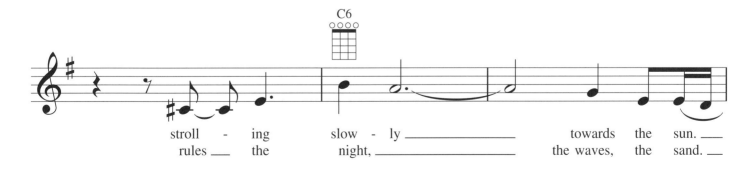

stroll - ing slow - ly _____ towards the sun. __
rules __ the night, _____ the waves, the sand. __

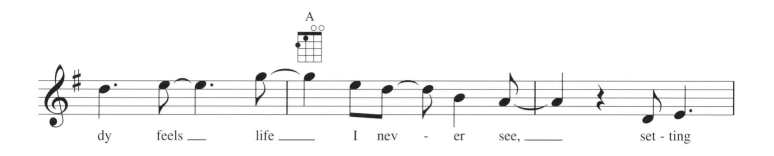

dy feels ___ life ___ I nev - er see, ___ set - ting

sons ___ and lone - ly lov - ers free. ___

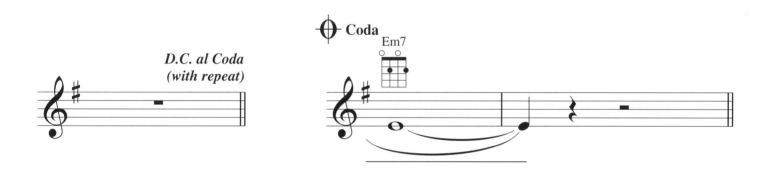

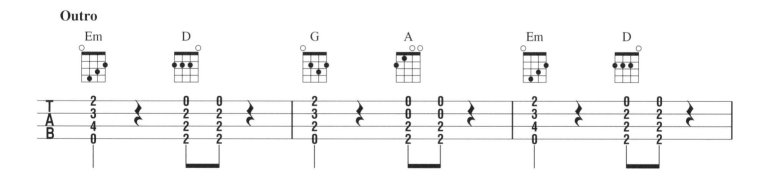

Outro

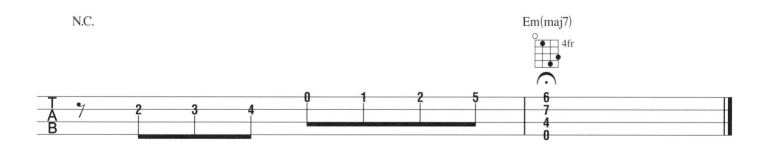

Help Me Make It Through the Night

Words and Music by Kris Kristofferson

First note

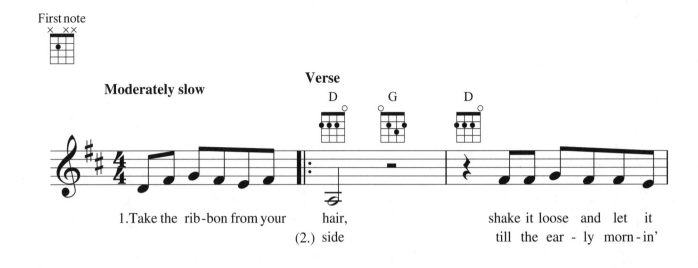

1. Take the rib-bon from your hair,
shake it loose and let it
(2.) side
till the ear - ly morn - in'

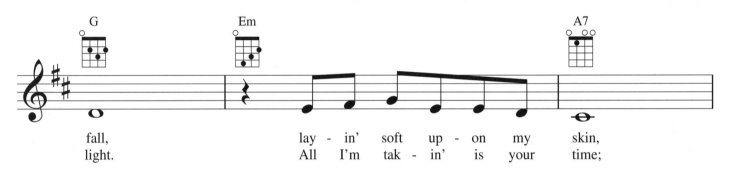

fall,
lay - in' soft up - on my skin,
light.
All I'm tak - in' is your time;

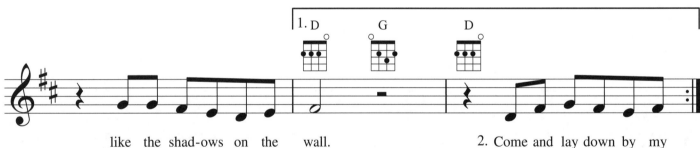

1. like the shad-ows on the wall.
help me make it through the

2. Come and lay down by my

2. night.

I don't care what's right or wrong.

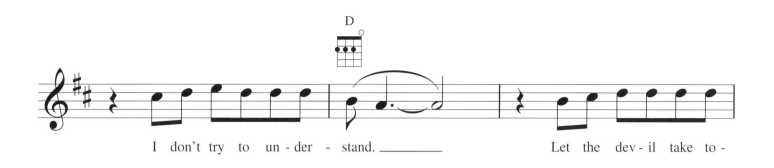

I don't try to un - der - stand. _____ Let the dev - il take to -

mor - row; _____ Lord, to - night I need a friend.

Outro-Verse

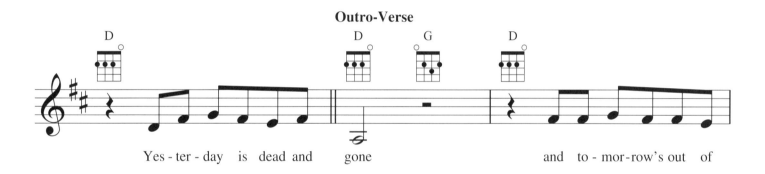

Yes - ter - day is dead and gone and to - mor-row's out of

sight, and it's sad to be a - lone;

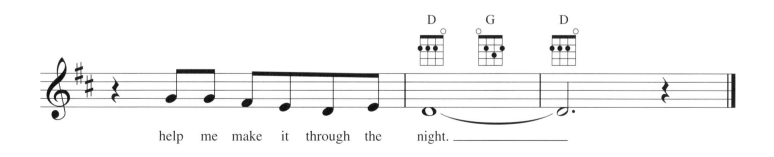

help me make it through the night. _____

(Hey, Won't You Play)
Another Somebody Done Somebody Wrong Song

Words and Music by Larry Butler and Chips Moman

First note

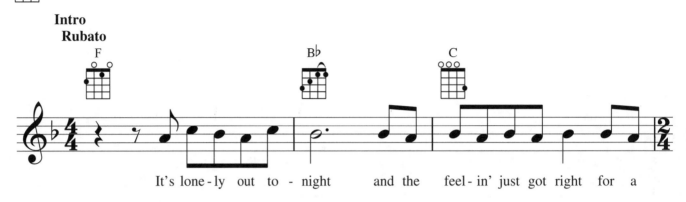

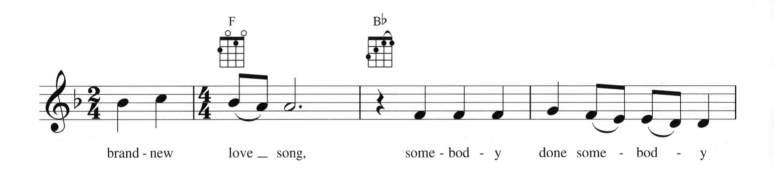

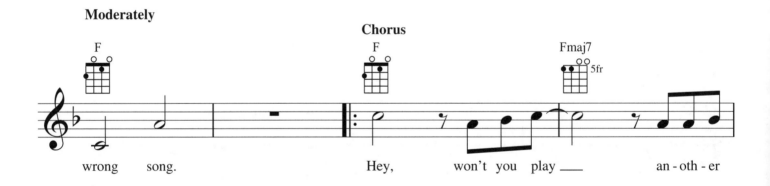

and make me feel at home while I miss my ba -

- by, while I miss my ba - by?

Verse

1., 2. So, play, play for me a sad mel - o - dy,

so sad that it makes ev - 'ry - bod - y

cry. A real hurt - in' song

a - bout a love that's gone wrong, 'cause

I don't __ want __ to cry ____ all a - lone. ___

Chorus

(1.) Hey,

(2., 3.) - by? Won't you play ____

won't you play ____

an - oth - er

some - bod - y done some - bod - y

wrong ___ song

and make me

feel ___ at home ___ while I miss my ba -

Play 3 times

- by, while I miss my ba - by?

(I Never Promised You A)
Rose Garden

Words and Music by Joe South

First note

Moderately fast

Chorus

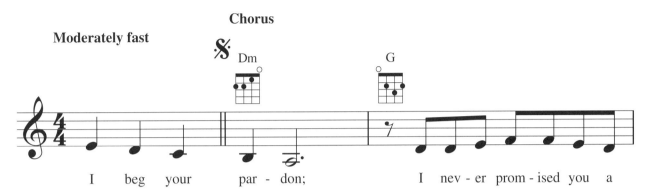

I beg your par-don; I nev-er prom-ised you a

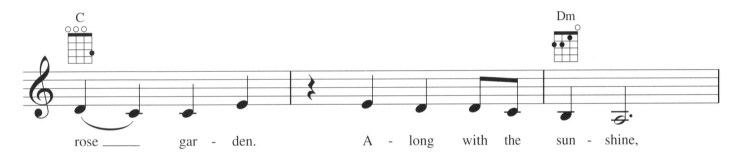

rose ___ gar-den. A-long with the sun-shine,

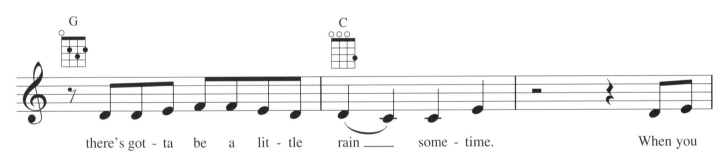

there's got-ta be a lit-tle rain ___ some-time. When you

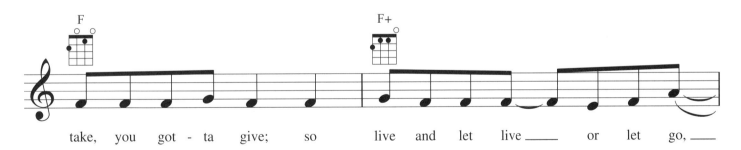

take, you got-ta give; so live and let live ___ or let go, ___

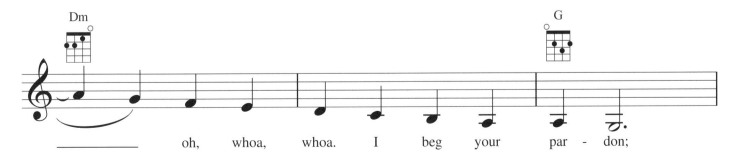

___ oh, whoa, whoa. I beg your par-don;

I nev - er prom-ised you a rose ___ gar - den. 1., 3. I could

Verse

prom - ise you things ___ like big dia - mond rings, ___ but you

2.–4. *See additional lyrics*

don't find ros - es grow-ing on stalks of clo - ver,

1., 3.

so you bet - ter think it o - ver. ___ 2. When it's

Bridge

2., 4.

So smile for a while and let's be jol - ly;

love should-n't be so mel - an - chol - y. Come a - long and share the good ___

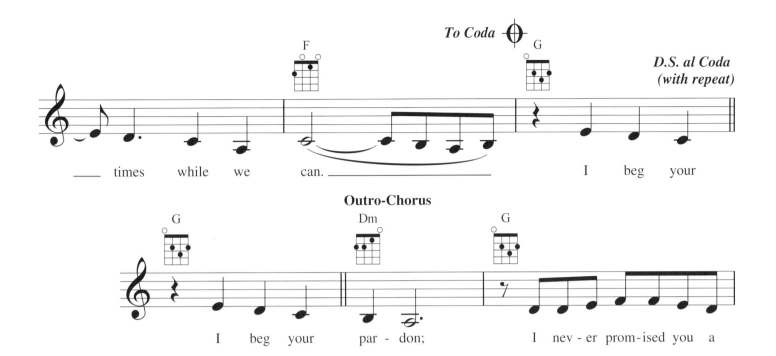

_____ times while we can. _____ I beg your

Outro-Chorus

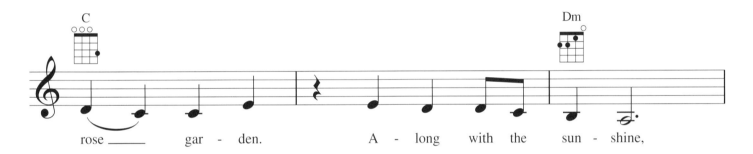

I beg your par - don; I nev - er prom-ised you a

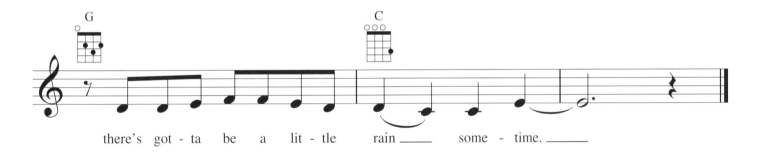

rose _____ gar - den. A - long with the sun - shine,

there's got - ta be a lit - tle rain _____ some - time. _____

Additional Lyrics

2. When it's sweet talking, you could make it come true,
   I would give you the world right now on a silver platter.
   But what would it matter?

3. I could sing you a tune and promise you the moon,
   But if that's what it takes to hold you, I'd just as soon let you go.
   But there's one thing I want you to know:

4. You better look before you leap; still waters run deep,
   And there won't always be someone there to pull you out,
   And you know what I'm talkin' about.

How Can You Mend a Broken Heart

Words and Music by Barry Gibb and Robin Gibb

First note

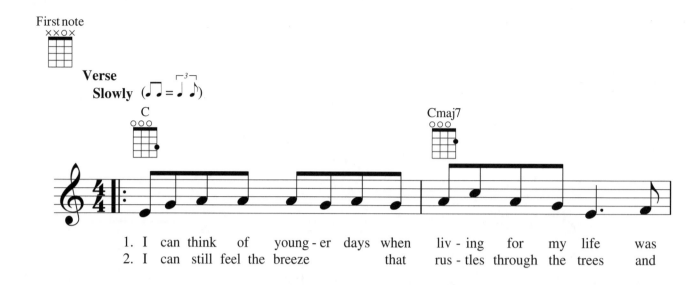

1. I can think of young-er days when liv-ing for my life was
2. I can still feel the breeze that rus-tles through the trees and

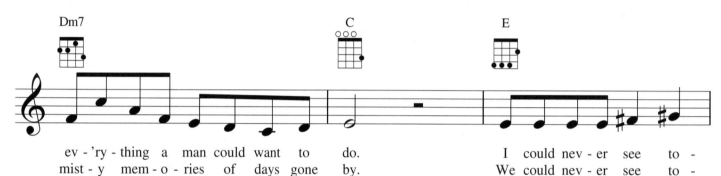

ev-'ry-thing a man could want to do.   I could nev-er see to-
mist-y mem-o-ries of days gone by.   We could nev-er see to-

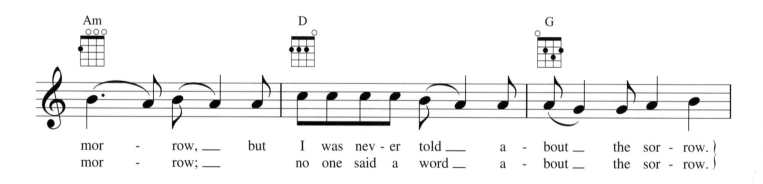

mor - row, ___ but I was nev-er told ___ a-bout ___ the sor-row.)
mor - row; ___ no one said a word ___ a-bout ___ the sor-row.)

Chorus

And   how can you mend ___ a bro-ken heart? ___

How can you stop the rain from fall - ing down?

How _____ can you stop the sun from shin - ing?

What makes the world go 'round? How can you mend _ this

bro - ken man? _ How can a los - er ev - er win? Please

help me mend my bro - ken heart and let me live a -

1. gain.

2. gain.

How Deep Is Your Love

from the Motion Picture SATURDAY NIGHT FEVER
Words and Music by Barry Gibb, Robin Gibb and Maurice Gibb

I Believe in Music

Words and Music by Mac Davis

long e - nough to sing a - long. _____ Ev - 'ry - bod - y sing:

Chorus

I be - lieve in mu - sic. ___

I _____ be - lieve in love.

D.S. al Coda

love. Sing it to me, chil - dren.

Coda

love.

Additional Lyrics

2. Music is love, love is music, if you know what I mean.
   People who believe in music are the happiest people I ever seen.
   So clap your hands, stomp your feet, shake your tambourine.
   Lift your voices to the sky. God loves you when you sing.

3. Music is the universal language and love is the key
   To brotherhood and peace and understanding to livin' in harmony.
   So take your brother by the hand and sing along with me.
   And find out what it really means to be young and rich and free.

A Horse with No Name

Words and Music by Dewey Bunnell

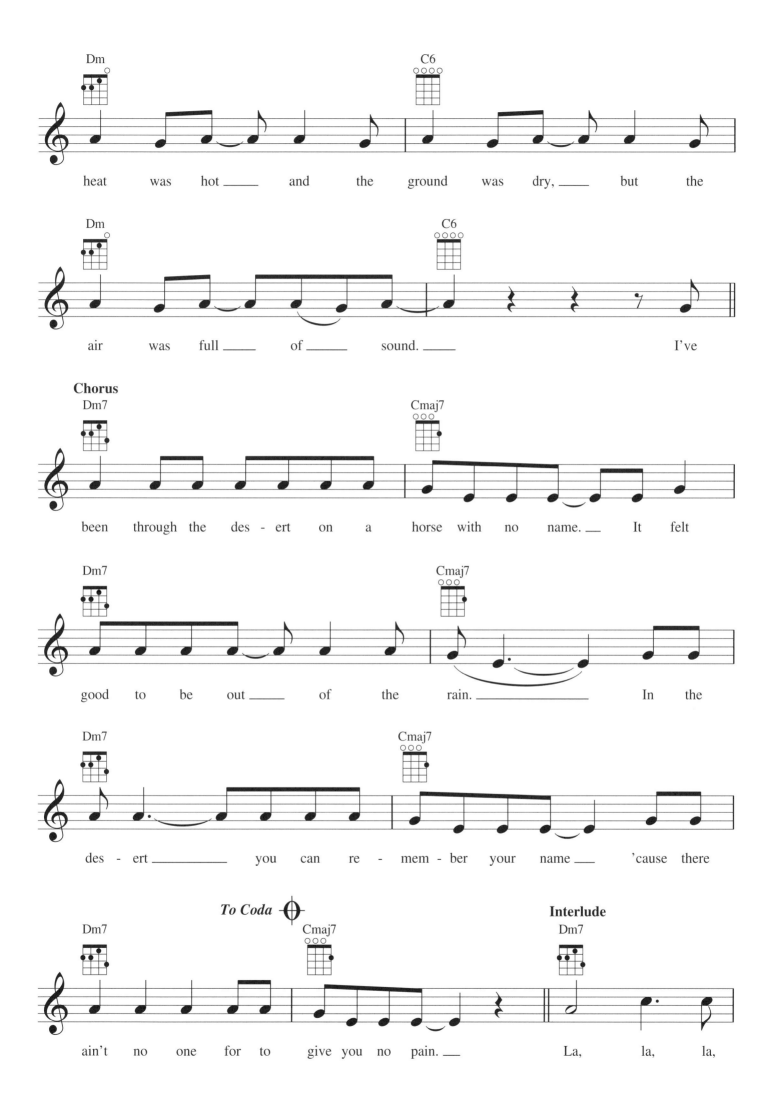

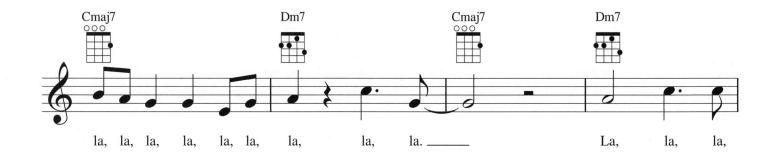

la, la, la, la, la, la, la, la, la. _____ La, la, la,

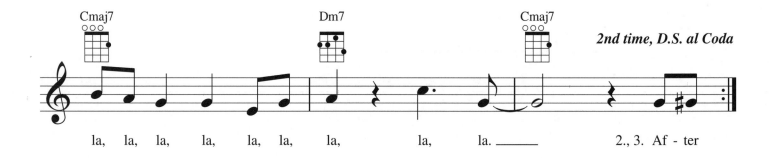

2nd time, D.S. al Coda

la, la, la, la, la, la, la, la, la. _____ 2., 3. Af - ter

Coda

Outro

give you no pain. ___ La, la, la, la,

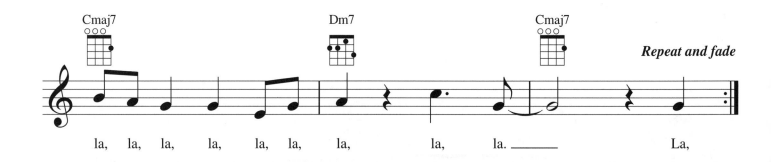

Repeat and fade

la, la, la, la, la, la, la, la, la. _____ La,

Additional Lyrics

2. After two days in the desert sun, my skin began to turn red.
   After three days in the desert fun, I was looking at a river bed.
   And the story it told of a river that flowed made me sad to think it was dead.
   (Skip to Chorus)

3. After nine days, I let the horse run free 'cause the desert had turned to sea.
   There were plants and birds and rocks and things, there were sand and hills and rings.
   The ocean is a desert with its life underground and the perfect disguise above.
   Under the cities lies a heart made of ground, but the humans will give no love.

If You Don't Know Me by Now

Words and Music by Kenneth Gamble and Leon Huff

First note

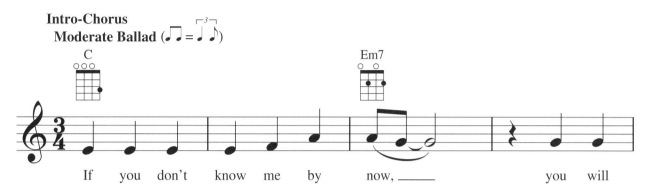

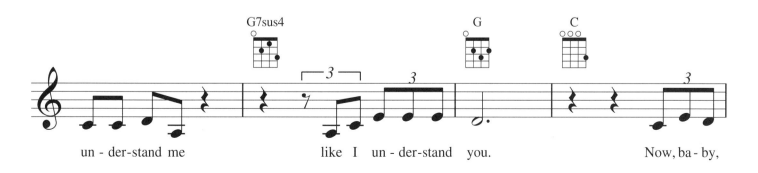

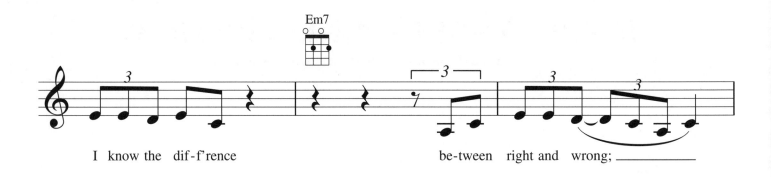

I know the dif-f'rence   be-tween right and wrong; _____

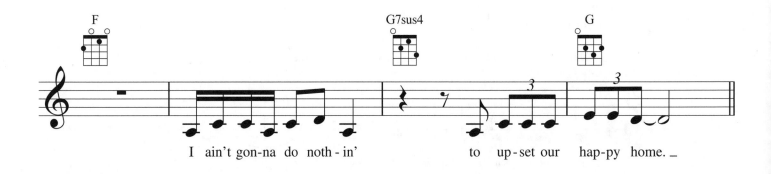

I ain't gon-na do noth-in'   to up-set our hap-py home. _

Pre-Chorus

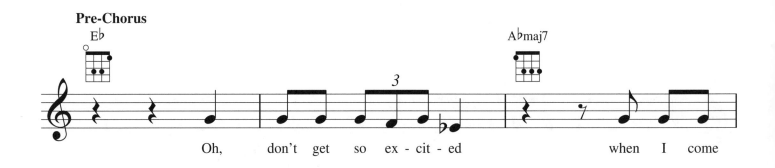

Oh,   don't get so ex-cit-ed   when I come

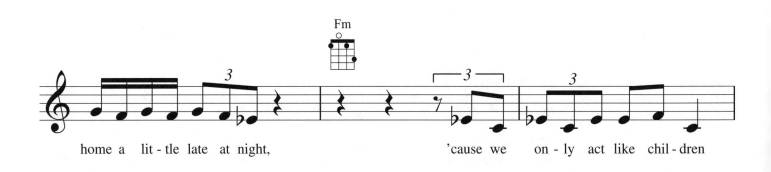

home a lit-tle late at night,   'cause we on-ly act like chil-dren

Chorus

when we ar-gue, fuss and fight. ___   If you don't know me by

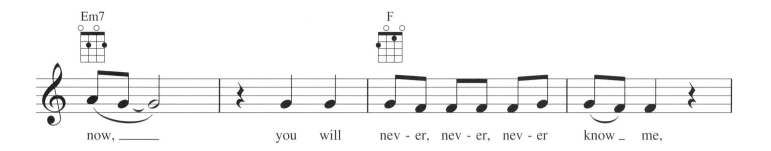

now, _____ you will nev - er, nev - er, nev - er know _ me,

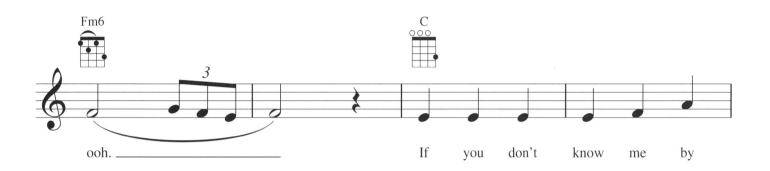

ooh. _____ If you don't know me by

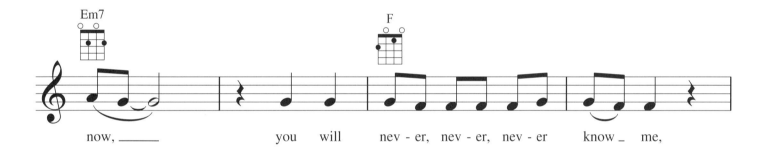

now, _____ you will nev - er, nev - er, nev - er know _ me,

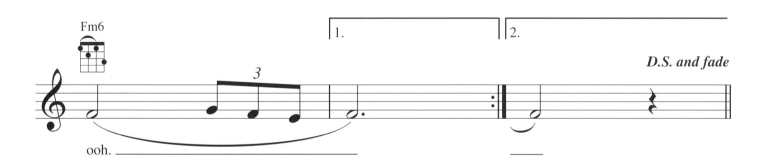

ooh. _____

Additional Lyrics

2. We all got our own funny moods.
   I've got mine; woman, you got yours, too.
   Just trust in me like I trust in you.
   As long as we've been together, that should be so easy to do.

Pre-Chorus: Just get yourself together, or we might as well say goodbye.
   What good is a love affair when we can't see eye to eye? Oh.

I Shot the Sheriff

Words and Music by Bob Marley

First note

Verse
Moderate Funk

1. I shot the sher - iff, but I did not shoot the
2.–5. *See additional lyrics*

dep - u - ty. I shot the sher - iff,

but I did - n't shoot the dep - u - ty.

All a - round in my home town, they're try - ing to track me down. ___

___ They say they want to bring me in guilt - y for the

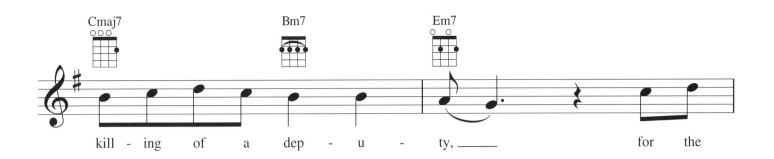

kill - ing   of   a   dep - u - ty, _____   for   the

life   of   a   dep - u - ty. __   But   I   say: __   *(Instrumental)*

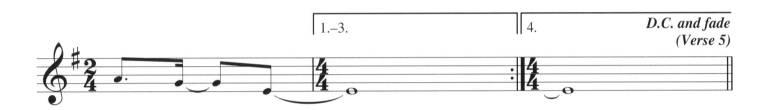

1.–3.   4.   ***D.C. and fade***
                                                     (Verse 5)

Additional Lyrics

2. I shot the sheriff, but I swear it was in self-defense.
   I shot the sheriff, and they say it is a capital offense.
   Sheriff John Brown always hated me; for what, I don't know.
   Every time that I plant a seed, he said, "Kill it before it grows."
   He said, "Kill it before it grows." But I say:

3. I shot the sheriff, but I swear it was in self-defense.
   I shot the sheriff, but I swear it was in self-defense.
   Freedom came my way one day, and I started out of town.
   All of a sudden, I see Sheriff John Brown aiming to shoot me down.
   So I shot, I shot him down. But I say:

4. I shot the sheriff, but I did not shoot the deputy.
   I shot the sheriff, but I did not shoot the deputy.
   Reflexes got the better of me, and what is to be must be.
   Every day, the bucket goes to the well, but one day the bottom will drop out.
   Yes, one day the bottom will drop out. But I say:

5. I shot the sheriff, but I didn't shoot the deputy.
   I shot the sheriff, but I did not shoot no deputy.
   Instrumental fade

I Think I Love You

featured in the Television Series THE PARTRIDGE FAMILY
Words and Music by Tony Romeo

First note

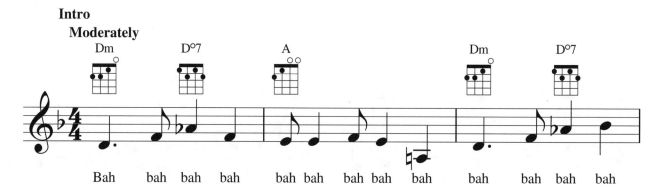

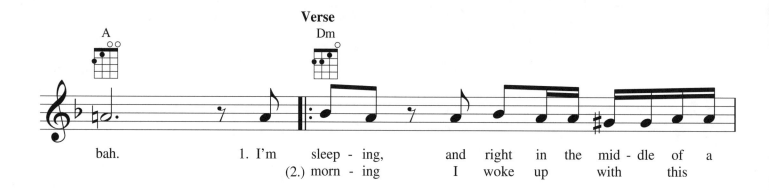

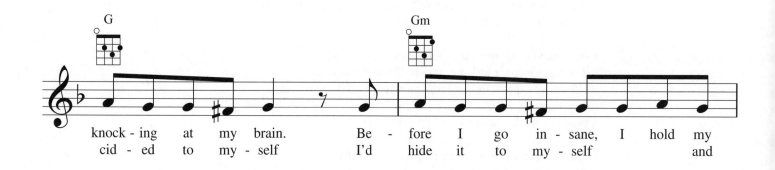

Outro-Verse

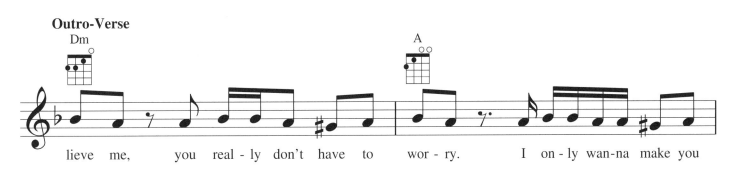

lieve me,   you real-ly don't have to   wor-ry.   I on-ly wan-na make you

hap-py,   and if you say, "Hey,   go a-way,"_ I will.   But

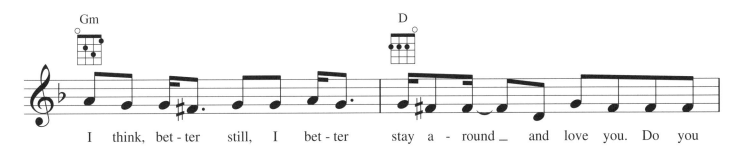

I think, bet-ter still, I bet-ter   stay a-round_ and love you. Do you

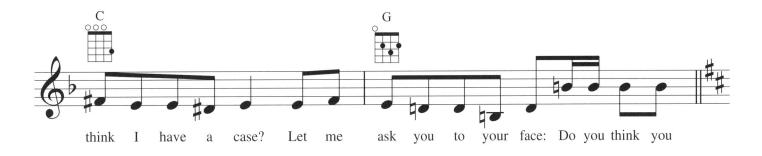

think I have a case? Let me   ask you to your face: Do you think you

love me?   I think I   love you.   I think I

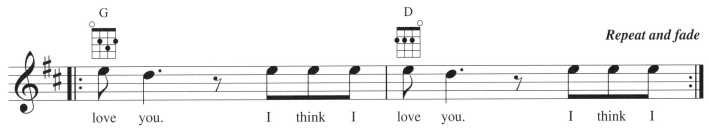

Repeat and fade

love you.   I think I   love you.   I think I

I'd Like to Teach the World to Sing

Words and Music by Bill Backer, Roquel Davis, Roger Cook and Roger Greenaway

1. I'd like to build __ the world __ a home __ and
2., 3. *See additional lyrics*

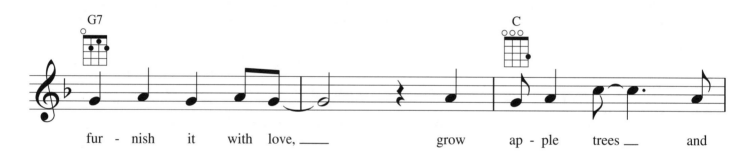

fur - nish it with love, __ grow ap - ple trees __ and

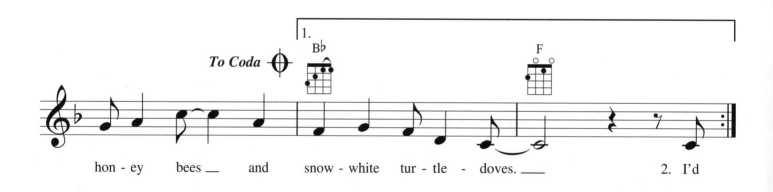

hon - ey bees __ and snow - white tur - tle - doves. __ 2. I'd

keep it com - pa - ny. __ 3. I'd

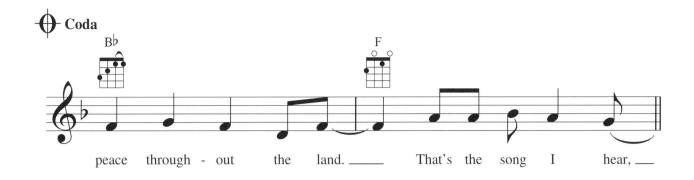

peace through - out the land. _____ That's the song I hear, ___

Bridge

_____ let the world sing to - day.

Outro

I'd like to teach ___ the world ___ to sing ___ in

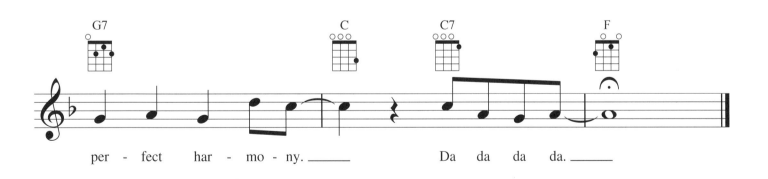

per - fect har - mo - ny. _____ Da da da da. _____

Additional Lyrics

2. I'd like to teach the world to sing in perfect harmony.
   I'd like to hold it in my arms and keep it company.

3. I'd like to see the world, for once, all standing hand in hand,
   And hear them echo through the hills for peace throughout the land.

If

Words and Music by David Gates

If You Could Read My Mind

Words and Music by Gordon Lightfoot

1. If you could read my mind, love,
2., 4. *See additional lyrics*
3. *Instrumental*

what a tale my thoughts could tell. Just like an old-

-time mov - ie 'bout a ghost from a wish - ing well.

Pre-Chorus

In a cas - tle dark or a for - tress strong, with chains
(3.) I'd walk a - way like a mov - ie star who gets

got to say ____ that I just don't get it.   I don't know ___ where we ___

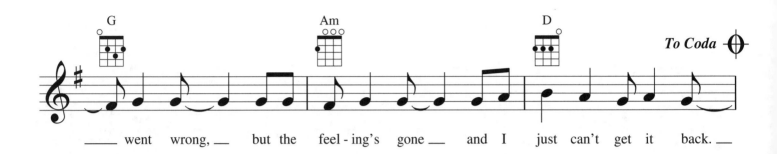

____ went wrong, ___ but the feel-ing's gone ___ and I just can't get it back. ___

To Coda ⊕

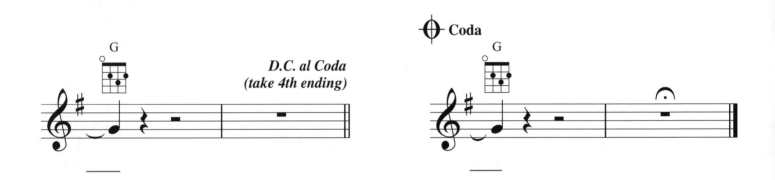

D.C. al Coda
(take 4th ending)

⊕ **Coda**

Additional Lyrics

2. If I could read your mind, love, what a tale your thoughts could tell.
   Just like a paperback novel, the kind the drug stores sell.
Pre-Chorus: When you reach the part where the heartaches come,
   The hero would be me, but heroes often fail.
   And you won't read that book again
   Because the ending's just too hard to take.

4. If you could read my mind, love, what a tale my thoughts could tell.
   Just like an old-time movie 'bout a ghost from a wishing well.
Pre-Chorus: In a castle dark or a fortress strong
   With chains upon my feet, but stories always end.
   And if you read between the lines,
   You'd know that I'm just trying to understand the feelings that you lack.

Imagine

Words and Music by John Lennon

(Instrumental)

1. I - mag-ine there's no heav - en, it's eas - y if you try; __

__ no hell __ be - low us,

a - bove us on - ly sky. __ I - mag-ine all the peo -

ple __ liv - ing for to - day, __ ah. __

Verse

2. I - mag - ine there's no coun - tries,
3. *See additional lyrics*

it is - n't hard ___ to do; ___

noth - ing to kill or die ___ for

and no re - li - gion, too. ___

I - mag - ine all the peo - ple ___

liv - ing life in peace. ___ You, ___

Chorus

you may say _____ I'm a dream-er, but I'm not the on-ly one. I hope some day _____ you'll join us _____ and the world _____ will

1. be as one. ____
2. live as one. ____

Additional Lyrics

3. Imagine no possessions,
   I wonder if you can;
   No need for greed or hunger,
   A brotherhood of man.
   Imagine all the people sharing all the world.

The Joker

Words and Music by Steve Miller, Eddie Curtis and Ahmet Ertegun

First note

Verse
Moderately

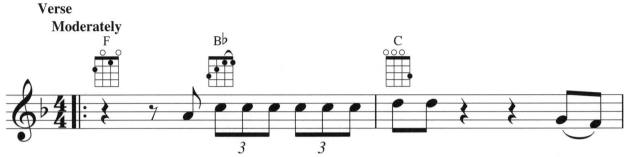

1. Some peo-ple call me the space cow-boy. Yeah! _
2. *See additional lyrics*

Some call me the gang-ster of love. _____

Some peo-ple call me Maur-ice _____ 'cause I

speak of the pom-pa-tus of love. _____

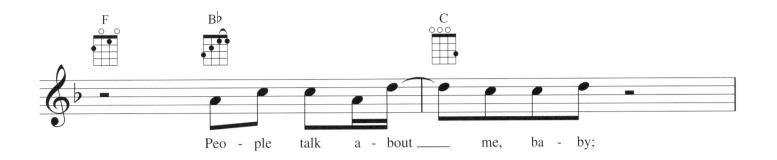

People talk a - bout ____ me, ba - by;

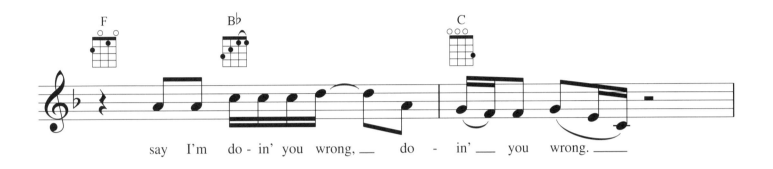

say I'm do - in' you wrong, __ do - in' __ you wrong. __

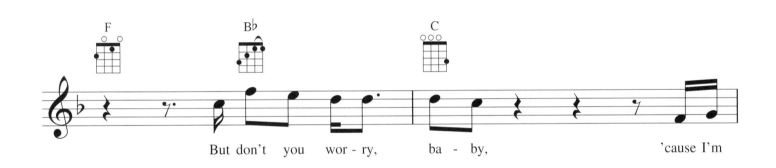

But don't you wor - ry, ba - by, 'cause I'm

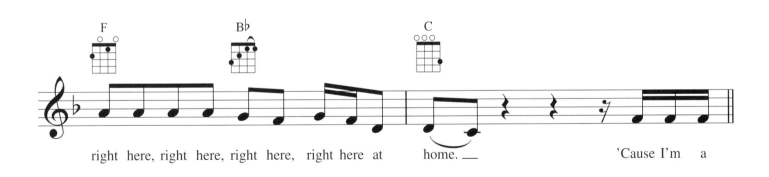

right here, right here, right here, right here at home. __ 'Cause I'm a

Chorus

pick-er, I'm a grin-ner, I'm a lov-er, and I'm a sin-ner.

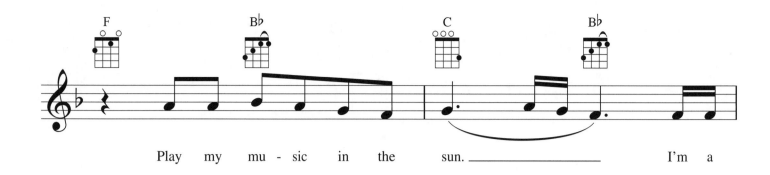

Play my mu - sic in the sun. _____ I'm a

jok - er, I'm a smok-er, I'm a mid - night _ tok - er.

I sure don't want to hurt no one. _____

Additional Lyrics

2. You're the cutest thing that I ever did see;
   I really love your peaches, want to shake your tree.
   Lovey dovey, lovey dovey, lovey dovey all the time;
   Ooh wee, baby, I'll sure show you a good time.

Lay Down Sally

Words and Music by Eric Clapton, Marcy Levy and George Terry

First note

Verse
Brightly

1. There is noth - ing that ____ is wrong ____ in
(2.) sun ain't near - ly on ____ the rise, ____ and
(3.) long to see ____ the morn - ing light ____

want - ing you ____ to stay ____ here ____ with me.
we still got ____ the moon and stars ____ a - bove.
col - or - ing ____ your face so dream - i - ly.

I know you've got ____ some - where ____ to go, ____ but
Un - der - neath ____ the vel - vet skies, ____
So don't you go ____ and say ____ good - bye; ____

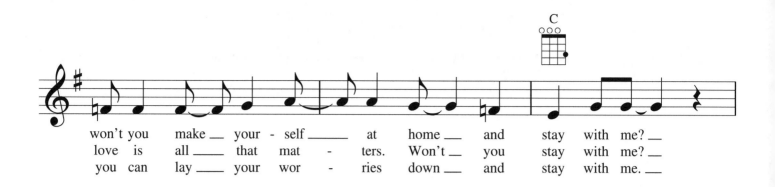

won't you make __ your - self _____ at home __ and stay with me? __
love is all ____ that mat - ters. Won't __ you stay with me? __
you can lay ___ your wor - ries down __ and stay with me. __

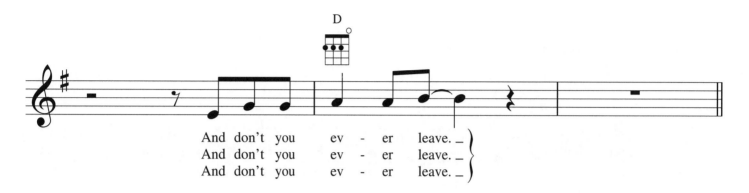

And don't you ev - er leave. _
And don't you ev - er leave. _
And don't you ev - er leave. _

𝄌 **Chorus**

Lay down, Sal - ly, and rest you in __ my arms. _

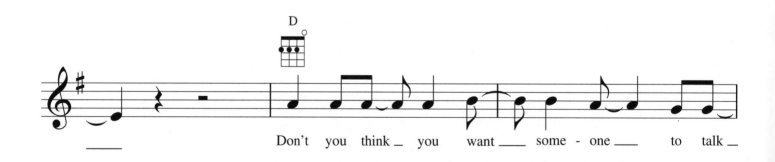

___ Don't you think __ you want ___ some - one __ to talk __

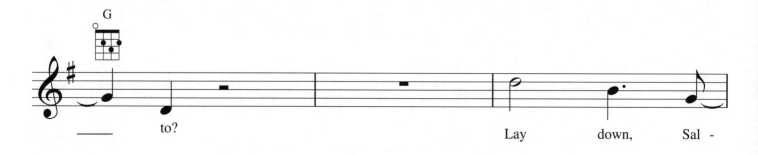

___ to? Lay down, Sal -

- ly;   no   need   to   leave __ so   soon. ____

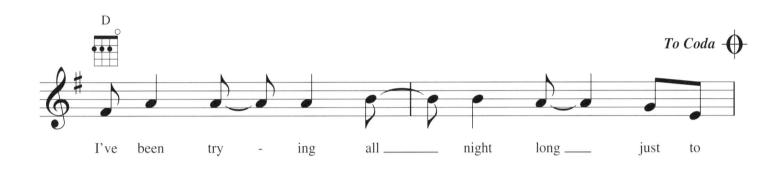

I've   been   try - ing   all ____ night   long __ just   to

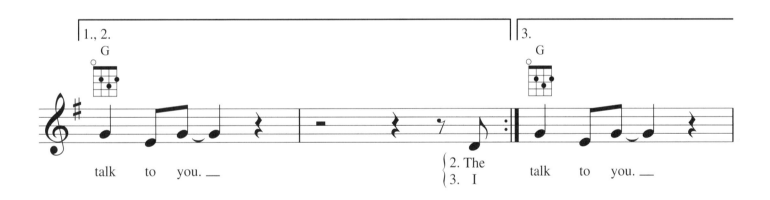

talk   to   you. __   2. The   talk   to   you. __
                                                        3. I

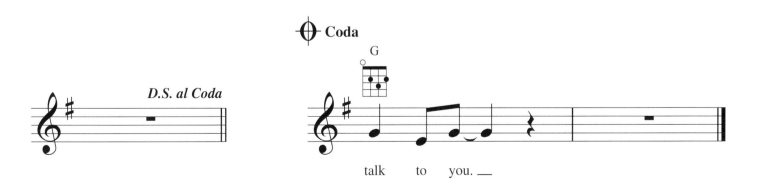

talk   to   you. __

Just the Way You Are

Words and Music by Billy Joel

Lady Marmalade

Words and Music by Bob Crewe and Kenny Nolan

Mo-cha choc-o-la-ta ya _____ ya. Cre-ole La-dy Mar-ma-lade. ___

Chorus 2

To Coda

Vou-lez vous cou-cher a-vec moi

ce soir? Vou-lez vous cou-cher a-vec moi?

1. **Verse**

2. Stayed in her bou-doir while she ___ fresh-ened up; ___ that boy drank all that mag-no-

-lia wine. On her black sat-in sheets, I swear ___ he start-ed to freak. ___

2. **Interlude**

(Instrumental)

Hey, ___ hey, ___ hey, _____ hey - ey - ey. __

Verse

__ 3. Seein' her skin, _ feel- in' silk - y smooth, col - or of ca - fé au lait, _
liv- in' his gray _ flan-nel life. _

__ made the ___ sav-age beast in-side roar un - til it cried, _ "More,
__ But when ___ he turns off to sleep, old ___ mem'ries keep... _ more,

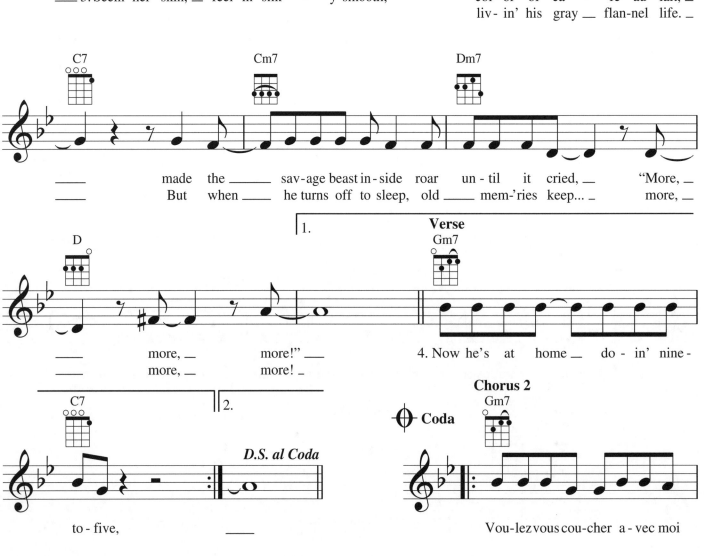

1.
__ more, _ more!" _
__ more, _ more! _

Verse

4. Now he's at home _ do- in' nine-

2.

D.S. al Coda

to - five, ___

Chorus 2

Coda

Vou- lez vous cou- cher a - vec moi

132

Laughter in the Rain

Words and Music by Neil Sedaka and Phil Cody

First note

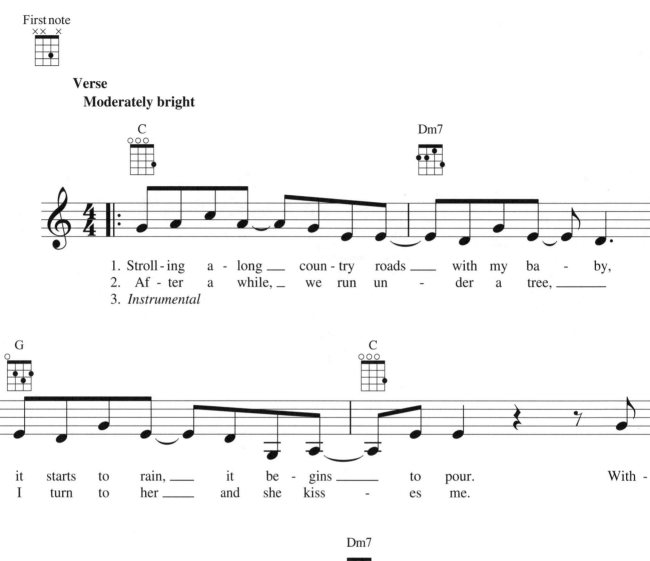

Verse
Moderately bright

1. Stroll-ing a - long ___ coun-try roads ___ with my ba - by,
2. Af - ter a while, ___ we run un - der a tree, _____
3. *Instrumental*

it starts to rain, ___ it be - gins _____ to pour. With -
I turn to her ___ and she kiss - es me.

out an um - brel - la we're soaked ___ to the skin, ___ I ___
There with the beat ___ of the rain _____ on the leaves, ___ soft -

___ feel a shiv - er run up _____ my spine.
- ly she breathes ___ and I close _____ my eyes,

End instrumental

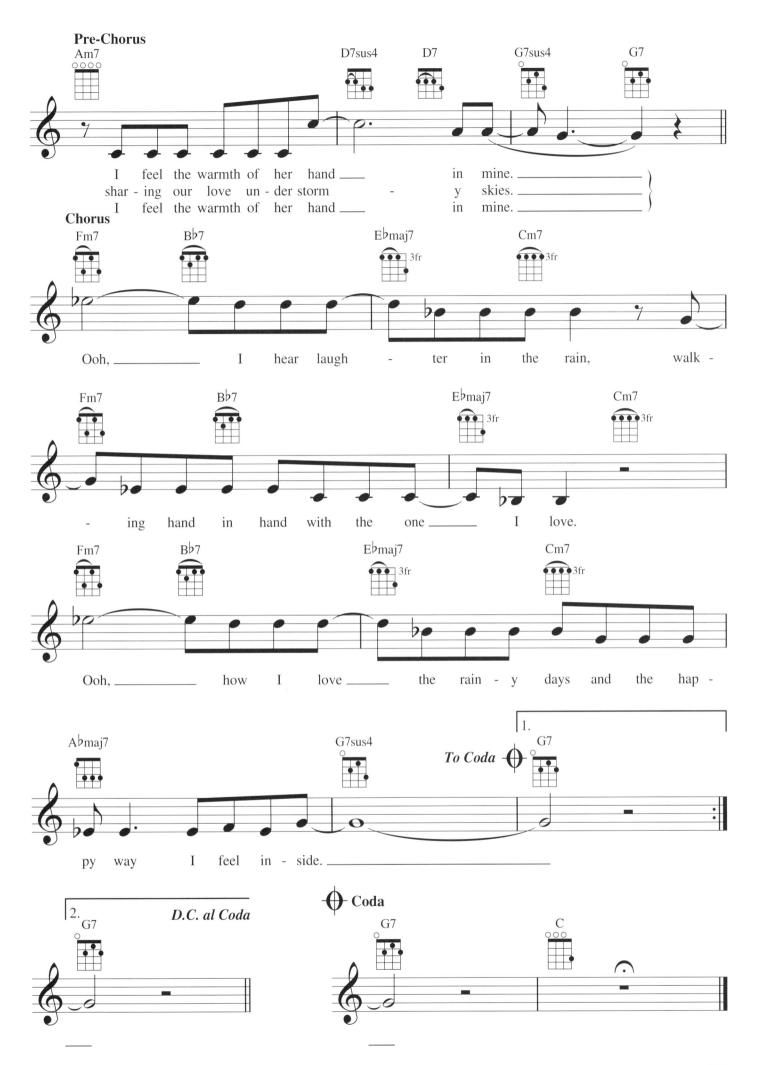

The Long and Winding Road

Words and Music by John Lennon and Paul McCartney

man-y times ___ I've cried. ___ An-y-way, ___ you'll nev-er know ___ the

Verse

man-y ways ___ I've tried. ___ And
Instrumental ends But { still they lead me back ___ to the long ___

___ wind-ing road. ___ You left me stand - ing here

a long, long time a-go. ___ Don't { leave / keep } me wait-

To Coda ⊕   *D.S. al Coda*

- ing here. Lead me to your ___ door.

⊕ **Coda**

door. Yeah, yeah, yeah, yeah. ___

Maggie May

Words and Music by Rod Stewart and Martin Quittenton

home, just to save you from be - ing a - lone. You

stole my heart, __ and that's what real - ly hurts.

1.–3.

4. **Outro**

2. The

(Instrumental)

Repeat and fade

Additional Lyrics

2. The morning sun, when it's in your face,
   Really shows your age.
   But that don't worry me none;
   In my eyes, you're everything.
   I laughed at all of your jokes.
   My love you didn't need to coax.
   Oh, Maggie, I couldn't have tried any more.

Chorus: You led me away from home
   Just to save you from being alone.
   You stole my soul,
   And that's a pain I can do without.

3. All I needed was a friend
   To lend a guiding hand.
   But you turned into a lover and, mother, what a lover!
   You wore me out.
   All you did was wreck my bed,
   And in the morning, kick me in the head.
   Oh, Maggie, I couldn't have tried any more.

Chorus: You led me away from home
   'Cause you didn't want to be alone.
   You stole my heart;
   I couldn't leave you if I tried.

4. I suppose I could collect my books
   And get on back to school,
   Or steal my daddy's cue
   And make a living out of playing pool.
   Or find myself a rock 'n' roll band
   That needs a helping hand.
   Oh, Maggie, I wish I'd never seen your face.

Chorus: You made a first-class fool out of me,
   But I'm as blind as a fool can be.
   You stole my heart, but I love you anyway.

Make It with You

Words and Music by David Gates

Margaritaville

Words and Music by Jimmy Buffett

1. Nib - blin' on sponge - cake, watch - in' the sun ___

2., 3. *See additional lyrics*

___ bake all of those tour - ists cov - ered with oil. ___

___ Strum - min' my six -

- string on my front porch ___ swing.

Smell those shrimp; ___ they're be - gin - ning to boil. ___

Additional Lyrics

2. Don't know the reason I stayed here all season
   With nothing to show but this brand-new tattoo.
   But it's a real beauty, a Mexican cutie.
   How it got here, I haven't a clue.

3. I blew out my flip-flop, stepped on a pop-top,
   Cut my heel, had to cruise on back home.
   But there's booze in the blender, and soon it will render
   That frozen concoction that helps me hang on.

Listen to the Music

Words and Music by Tom Johnston

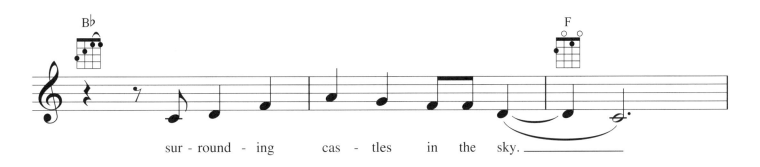

sur - round - ing   cas - tles   in   the   sky. _____

And the   crowd   is   grow - ing   big - ger,

lis - t'ning   for   the   hap - py   sounds, __   and   I

D.S. al Coda

Coda

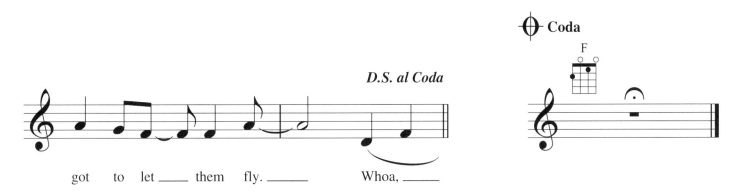

got   to   let ___ them   fly. _____   Whoa, _____

Additional Lyrics

2. What the people need is a way to make them smile.
   It ain't so hard to do if you know how.
   Got to get a message, get it on through.
   Oh, now mama's going to after 'while.

3. Well, I know you know better everything I say.
   Meet me in the country for a day.
   We'll be happy and we'll dance.
   Oh, we're gonna dance our blues away.

4. If I'm feeling good to you and you're feeling good to me,
   There ain't nothing we can't do or say.
   Feeling good, feeling fine.
   Oh, baby, let the music play.

Moondance

Words and Music by Van Morrison

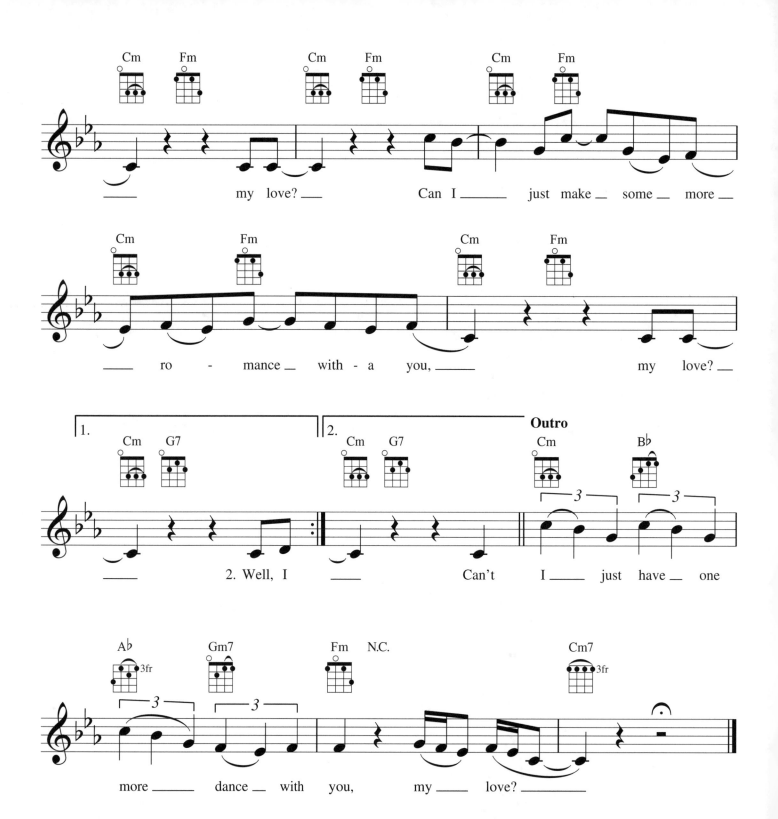

Additional Lyrics

2. Well, I wanna make love to you tonight; I can't wait till the morning has come.
   And I know now the time is just right, and straight into my arms you will run.
   And when you come, my heart will be waiting to make sure that you're never alone.
   There and then all my dreams will come true, dear; there and then I will make you my own.

   Pre-Chorus:
   And ev'ry time I touch you, you just tremble inside,
   And I know how much you want me that you can't hide.

Maybe I'm Amazed

Words and Music by Paul McCartney

First note

Verse
Moderately, in 2

1. Ba- by, I'm a - mazed at the way you love me all ___ the time, ___
2. *Instrumental*
3. *See additional lyrics*

___ and may - be I'm a - fraid of the way I love ___

___ you. *(Instrumental)* Ba - by, I'm a-

mazed at the way you pulled me out ___ of time. ___ You

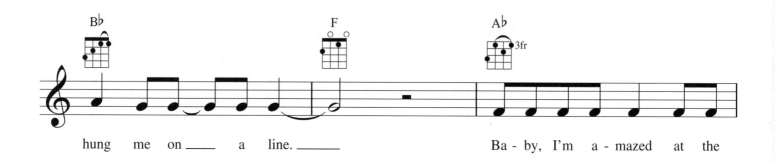

hung me on _____ a line. _____   Ba - by, I'm a - mazed at the

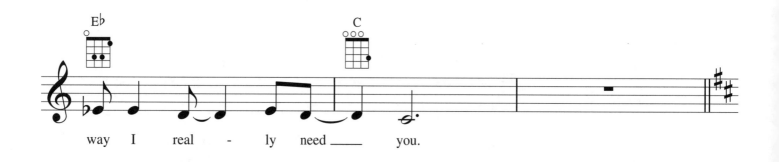

way I real - ly need _____ you.

𝄋 Chorus

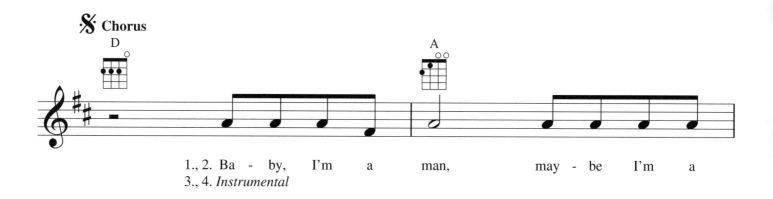

1., 2. Ba - by, I'm a man,   may - be I'm a
3., 4. *Instrumental*

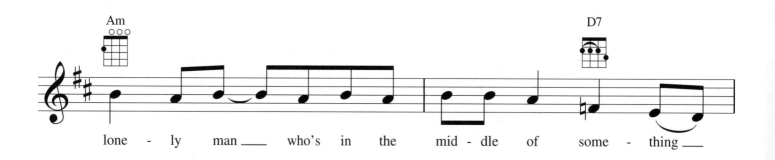

lone - ly man _____ who's in the mid - dle of some - thing _____

that he does - n't real - ly un - der - stand.

Additional Lyrics

3. Maybe I'm amazed at the way you're with me all the time.
Maybe I'm afraid of the way I need you.
Baby, I'm amazed at the way you help me sing my song,
Right me when I'm wrong.
Baby, I'm amazed at the way I really need you.

Me and You and a Dog Named Boo

Words and Music by Lobo

1. I re - mem - ber to ___ this day ___ the bright ___

2., 3. See additional lyrics

___ red Geor - gia clay, ___ and how it stuck ___ to the tires ___

___ af - ter the sum - mer rain. Will -

pow - er made that old car go; ___ a wom - an's

mind told me that's so. ___ Oh, how I wish ___ we were

back on the road ___ a - gain. ___

Chorus

Me and you ___ and a dog ___ named Boo, ___

trav -'lin' and a - liv - in' off the land. Me and you ___ and a dog ___

___ named Boo; ___ how I love ___ be - in' a free man.

3. F

D.S. al Coda

Coda F

2. Now, man.
3. Now, I'll

man.

Additional Lyrics

2. Now, I can still recall the wheat fields of St. Paul
And the mornin' we got caught robbin' from an old hen.
Old MacDonald, he made us work, but then he paid us for what it was worth.
Another tank of gas and back on the road again.

3. Now, I'll never forget the day we motored stately into big L. A.
The lights of the city put settlin' down in my brain.
Though it's only been a month or so, that old car's buggin' us to go.
We gotta get away and get back on the road again.

My Love

Words and Music by Paul McCartney and Linda McCartney

157

my love. On-ly my love ___ does it good to _____

me. Wo wo wo wo wo _____ wo _____ wo.

Additional Lyrics

2. And when the cupboard's bare,
   I'll still find something there with my love;
   It's understood.
   It's everywhere with my love,
   And my love does it good.

3. Don't ever ask me why
   I never say goodbye to my love;
   It's understood.
   It's everywhere with my love,
   And my love does it good.

One Toke Over the Line

Words and Music by Michael Brewer and Thomas E. Shipley

One toke o - ver the line, _____ sweet Je - sus,
one toke o - ver the line, _____ sweet Je - sus,

one toke o - ver the line. _____

Sit - tin' down - town in a rail - way sta - tion,

one toke o - ver the line. _____

Wait - in' for the train that goes home, sweet Mar - y,

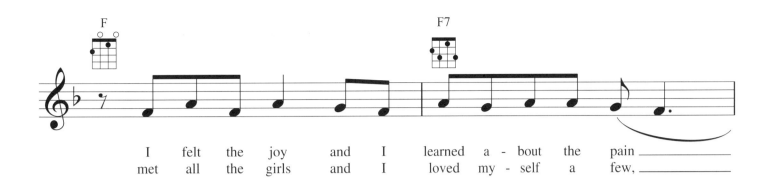

I felt the joy and I learned a - bout the pain _____
met all the girls and I loved my - self a few, _____

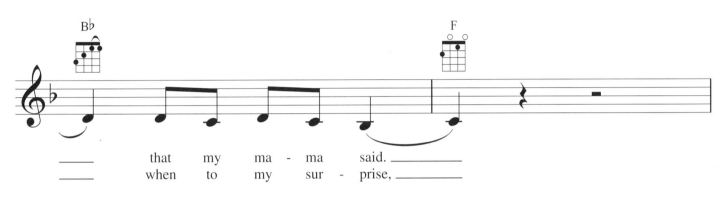

_____ that my ma - ma said. _____
_____ when to my sur - prise, _____

If I should choose to make a part of me, _____
like ev - 'ry - thing else that I've been through, _____

2nd time, D.C. al Coda

would sure - ly strike me dead. _____ And now I'm
it o - pened up my eyes. _____

_____ One _____ toke, one toke o - ver the line. _____

New World Coming

Words and Music by Barry Mann and Cynthia Weil

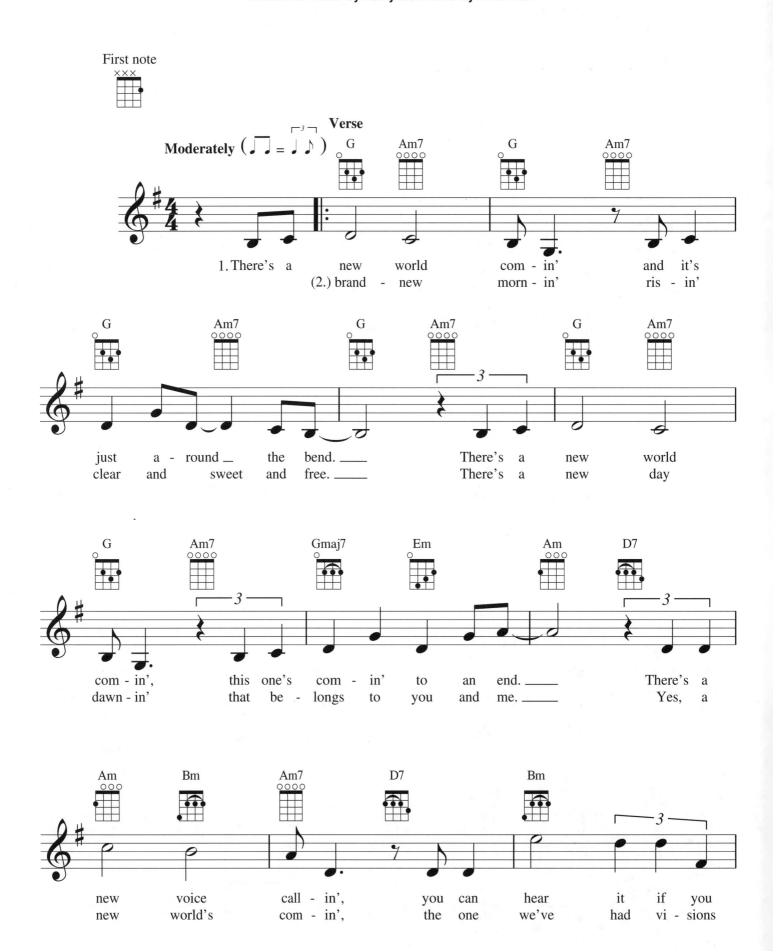

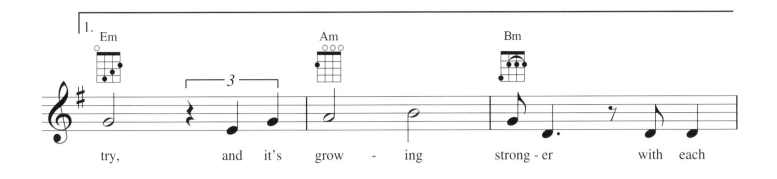

try, and it's grow - ing strong - er with each

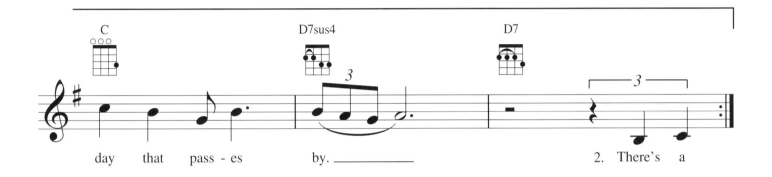

day that pass - es by. _____ 2. There's a

of, com - in' in peace, com - in' in joy, com - in' in ____

Outro

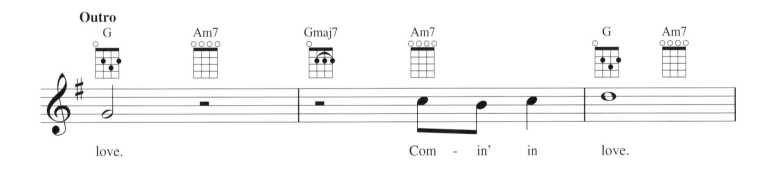

love. Com - in' in love.

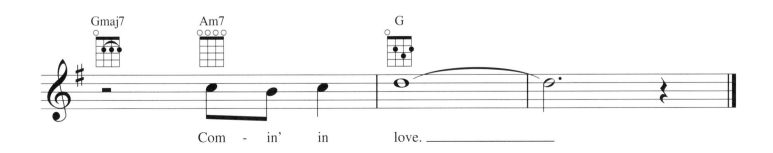

Com - in' in love. _____

Nights in White Satin

Words and Music by Justin Hayward

First note

Verse

Moderately slow, in 2

1. Nights in white sat-in, _____ nev-er reach-ing the
2. Gaz-ing at peo-ple, _____ some hand in

end. Let-ters I've writ-ten, _____
hand; just what I'm go-ing through,

nev-er mean-ing to send. _____
they can't un-der-stand. _____

Verse

Beau-ty I'd al-ways missed
Some try to tell me _____

with these eyes _____ be-fore.
thoughts they can-not de-fend.

Just what the
Just what you

Peaceful Easy Feeling

Words and Music by Jack Tempchin

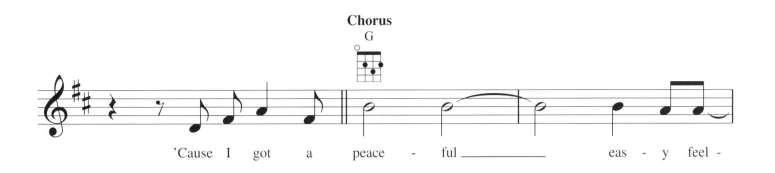

Chorus

'Cause I got a peace - ful _____ eas - y feel -

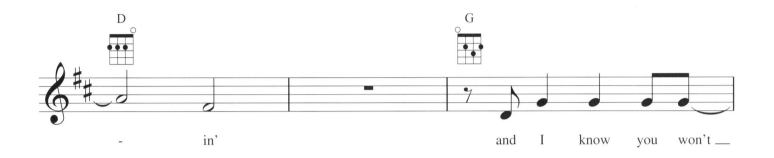

- in' and I know you won't ___

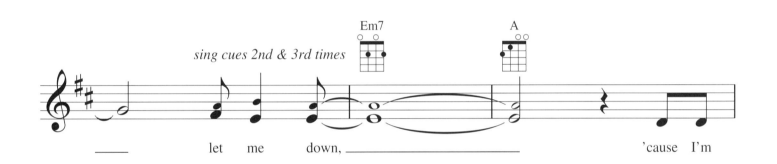

sing cues 2nd & 3rd times

___ let me down, _____ 'cause I'm

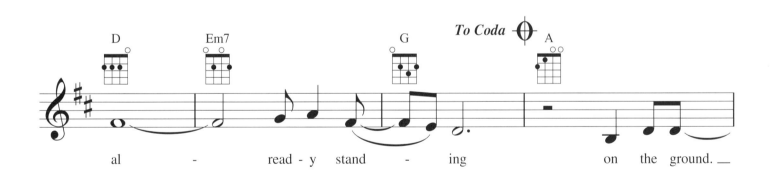

al - read - y stand - ing on the ground. __

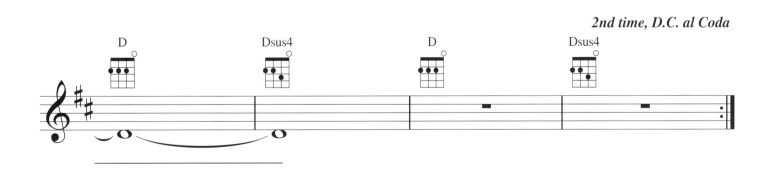

2nd time, D.C. al Coda

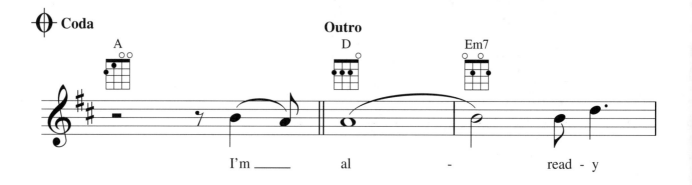

I'm _____ al - read - y

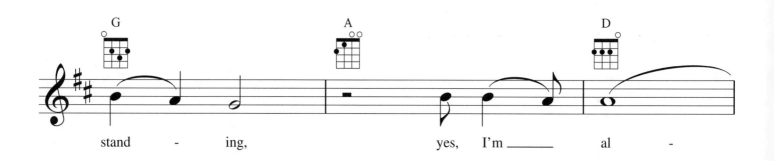

stand - ing, yes, I'm _____ al -

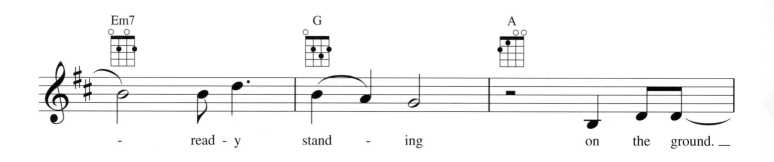

- read - y stand - ing on the ground. _

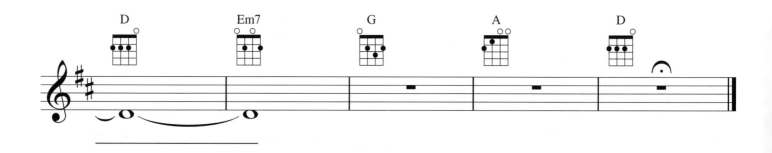

Additional Lyrics

2. And I found out a long time ago
   What a woman can do to your soul.
   Ah, but she can't take you any way
   You don't already know how to go.
   And I got a... *(To Chorus)*

3. I get this feeling I may know you
   As a lover and a friend.
   But this voice keeps whispering in my other ear;
   Tells me I may never see you again.
   'Cause I get a... *(To Chorus)*

Rocky Mountain High

Words and Music by John Denver and Mike Taylor

you might say he found a key ___ for ev - 'ry door. ___
and he lost a friend but kept his mem - o - ry. ___

%: **Verse**

___ 2. When he first came to the moun -
___ 4. Now he walks in qui - et sol -
(5.) ___ is full of won -

- tains, ___ his life ___ was far a - way, ___ on the road ___
- i - tude, the for - ests and the streams ___ seek - ing
- der ___ but his heart ___ still knows some fear ___ of a

___ and hang - in' by a song. ___
grace ___ in ev - 'ry step he takes. ___
sim - ple thing he can - not com - pre - hend: ___

___ But the string's al - read - y bro - ken and he
___ His sight ___ has turned in - side ___ him - self to
___ Why they try to tear the moun - tains down to

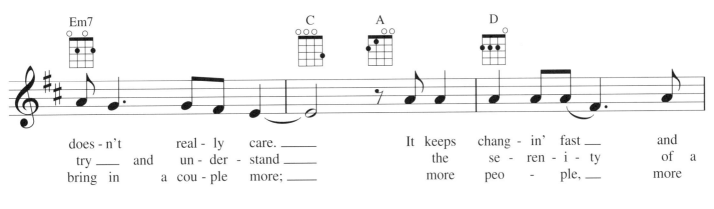

does-n't really care. _____ It keeps chang-in' fast _____ and
try _____ and un - der - stand _____ the se - ren - i - ty of a
bring in a cou - ple more; _____ more peo - ple, _____ more

it don't last _____ for long. _____ But the
clear blue moun - tain lake. _____ And the
scars up - on _____ the land. _____ And the

Chorus

Col - o - ra - do Rock - y Moun - tain high, _____

I've seen it rain - in' fire _____ in _____ the sky. _____

_____ The shad - ow from the star -
Talk to God and
I know he'd be a poor -

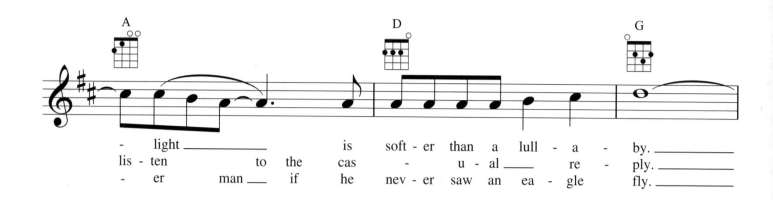

- light _____ is soft - er than a lull - a - by. _____
lis - ten to the cas - u - al ____ re - ply. _____
- er man ___ if he nev - er saw an ea - gle fly. _____

Rock - y Moun - tain high. __

_____ (Instrumental)

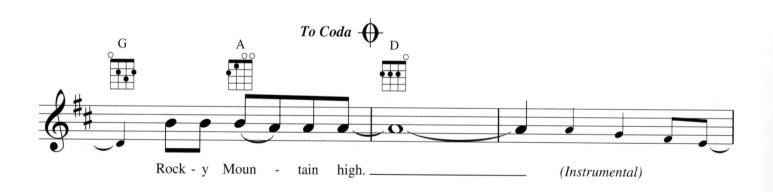

Rock - y Moun - tain high. _____ (Instrumental)

3. He climbed ___   5. Now his life ___

Please Come to Boston

Words and Music by Dave Loggins

1. He said, "Please come to Bos - ton for ___ the spring - time.
2., 3. *See additional lyrics*

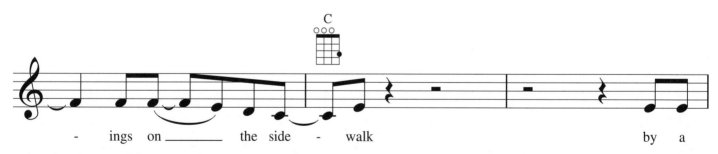

I'm stay - ing here ___ with some friends ___ and they've ___ got lots ___ ___ of room.

You can sell your paint -

- ings on ___ the side - walk by a

ca - fé where I hope ___ to be work - in' soon. ___

Please come to Bos - ton." She ___ said, "No, ___ boy, would

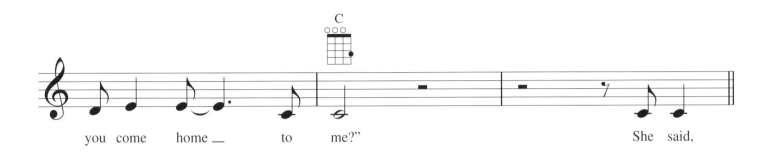

you come home ___ to me?" She said,

Chorus

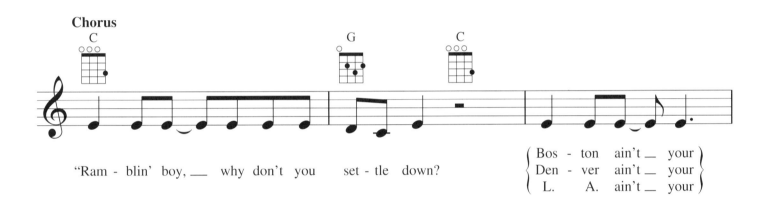

"Ram - blin' boy, ___ why don't you set - tle down?

{ Bos - ton ain't ___ your }
{ Den - ver ain't ___ your }
{ L. A. ain't ___ your }

kind of town. ___ There ain't no gold ___ and there ain't ___ no - bod ___ y like

me. _____ I'm the num - ber one fan of the man ___

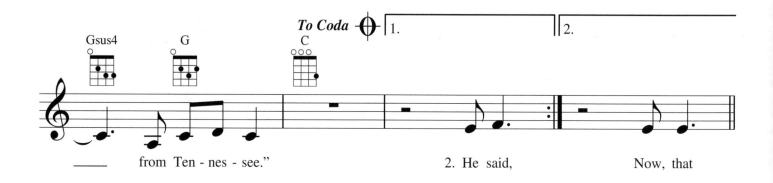

from Ten - nes - see."   2. He said,   Now, that

Bridge

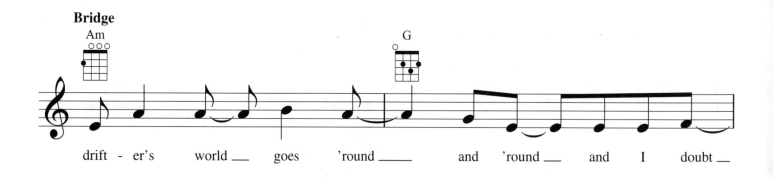

drift - er's   world   goes   'round   and   'round   and   I   doubt

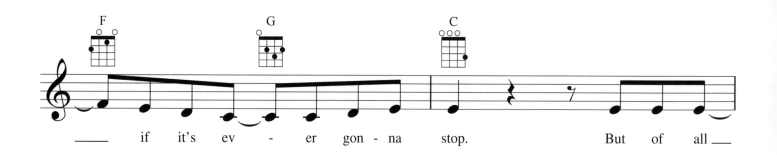

if   it's   ev - er   gon - na   stop.   But   of   all

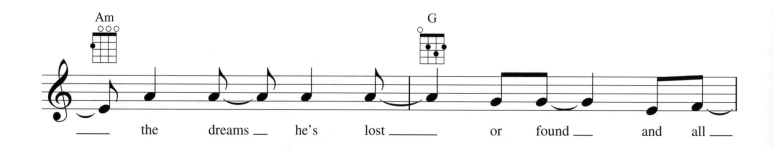

the   dreams   he's   lost   or   found   and   all

that   I   ain't   got,   he   still   needs   to   lean   to

some - bod - y he can sing to. ____ He said,

I'm the num - ber one fan of the man ____

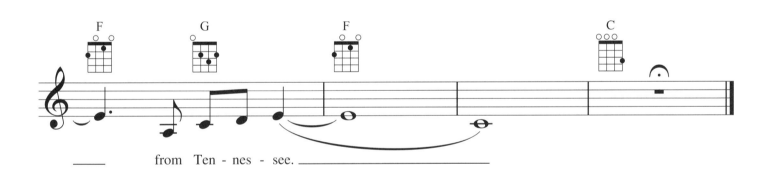

____ from Ten - nes - see. ____

Additional Lyrics

1. "Please come to Denver with the snowfall.
   We'll move up into the mountains so far we can't be found,
   And throw "I love you" echoes down the canyons,
   And then lie awake at night until they come back around.
   Please come to Denver." She just said, "No, boy, won't you come home to me?"

2. "Please come to L.A. to live forever.
   A California life alone is just too hard to build.
   I live in a house that looks out over the ocean,
   And there's some stars that fell from the sky livin' up on the hill.
   Please come to L.A." She just said, "No, boy, won't you come home to me?"

Reunited

Words and Music by Dino Fekaris and Freddie Perren

re - gret the mo - ment that I let you go. _____ Our

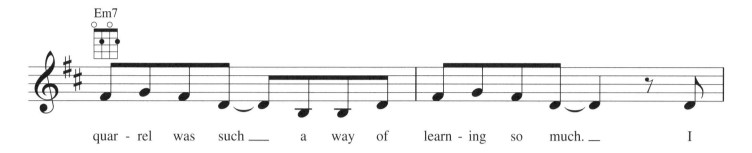

quar - rel was such ___ a way of learn - ing so much. __ I

know now that I love you 'cause I need your touch, _ hey, ___ hey! __

Chorus

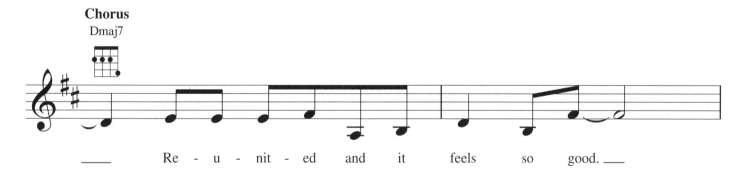

_____ Re - u - nit - ed and it feels so good. ___

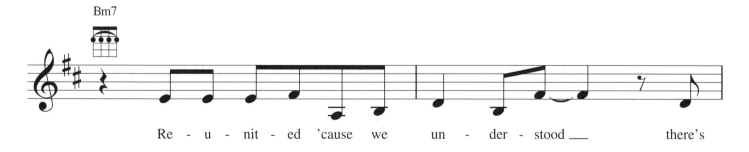

Re - u - nit - ed 'cause we un - der - stood ___ there's

one per - fect fit _____ and, sug - ar, this one is it. _____ We

both   are   so   ex - cit - ed   'cause we're   re - u - nit - ed,   hey, ___   hey! __

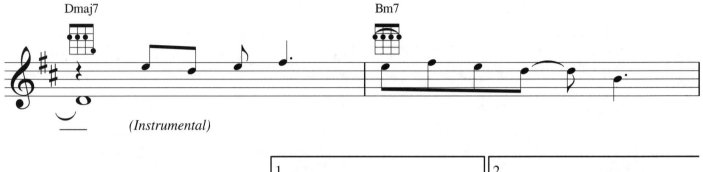

(Instrumental)

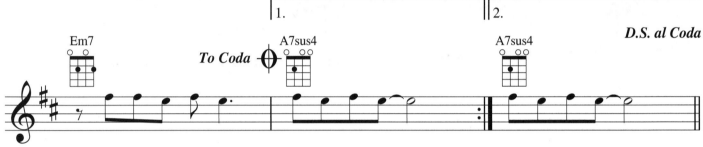

D.S. al Coda

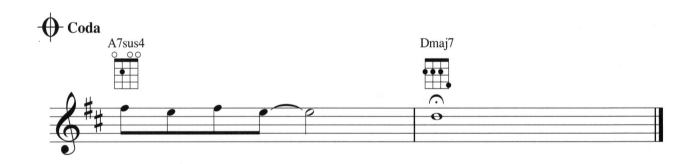

Additional Lyrics

4. I can't go cheatin', honey, I can't play.
   I found it very hard to stay away.
   As we reminisce on precious moments like this,
   I'm glad we're back together 'cause I missed your kiss, hey, hey!

5. Lover, lover, this is solid love,
   And you're exactly what I'm dreaming of.
   All through the day and all through the night,
   I'll give you all the love I have with all my might, hey, hey!

She Believes in Me

Words and Music by Steve Gibb

light. _____ Then qui-et-ly _____ she says, ___ "How was your
two. _____ Then I'm torn be-tween ___ the things ___ that I should

night?" And I come to her ___ and say, _____ "It was all
do. Then she says to wake ___ her up _____ when I am

right." And I hold her tight. ___
through. *(Spoken:) God, her love is true.* And she be-

Chorus

lieves in me. I'll nev-er know ___ just what she

sees in me. ___ I told her some-day, ___ if she

was my girl, ___ I could change ___ the world ___ with my

Right Time of the Night

Words and Music by Peter McCann

First note

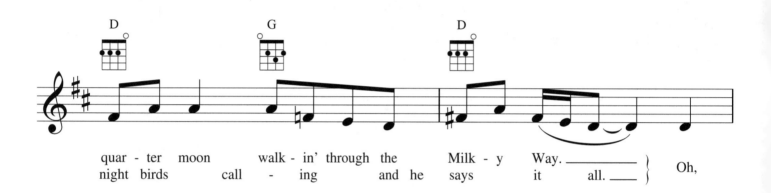

Teach Your Children

Words and Music by Graham Nash

Chorus

Teach your chil - dren well;
Teach your par - ents well;

their fa - ther's hell did slow - ly go ___
their chil - dren's hell will slow - ly go ___

___ by.
___ by. And feed

them on ___ your dreams; the one ___ they

pick's the one ___ you'll know ___ by. _____

___ Don't you ev - er ask ___ them

188

why; if they told you, you ___ would { die, / cry, } so just

look at them ___ and sigh _____

1.
and know they love _____ you.

*Let chord ring.

2.
2. And love _____ you.

*Let chord ring.

Additional Lyrics

2. And you of tender years
   Can't know the fears that your elders grew by.
   And so, please help them with your youth.
   They seek the truth before they can die.

Silly Love Songs

Words and Music by Paul McCartney and Linda McCartney

like to know, _____ 'cause here I go _____

Chorus

____ a - gain. _____ I

love you. you.

Verse

2. Ah, _____ I can't ex - plain; _____ the feel-ing's plain to me. Now,

can't you see? Ah, she gave me more, _____ she gave it

Pre-Chorus

all to me. Now, can't you see? What's wrong with that? _____

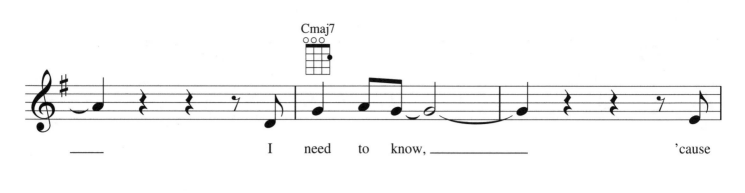

I need to know, _____ 'cause

here I go _____ a - gain. _____

Chorus

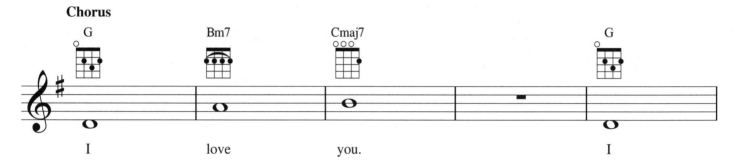

I love you. I

Bridge

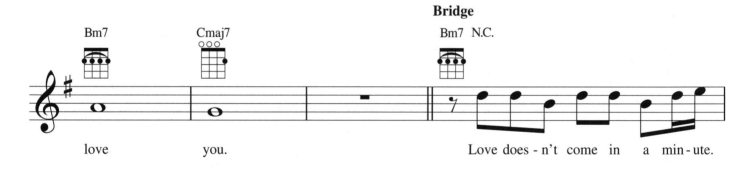

love you. Love does-n't come in a min-ute.

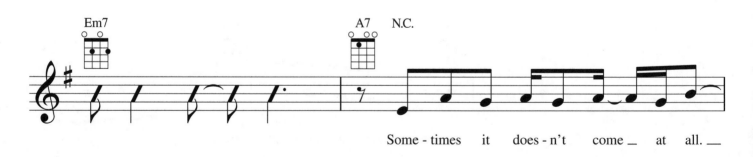

Some - times it does-n't come _ at all. _

I on - ly know that when I'm in it,

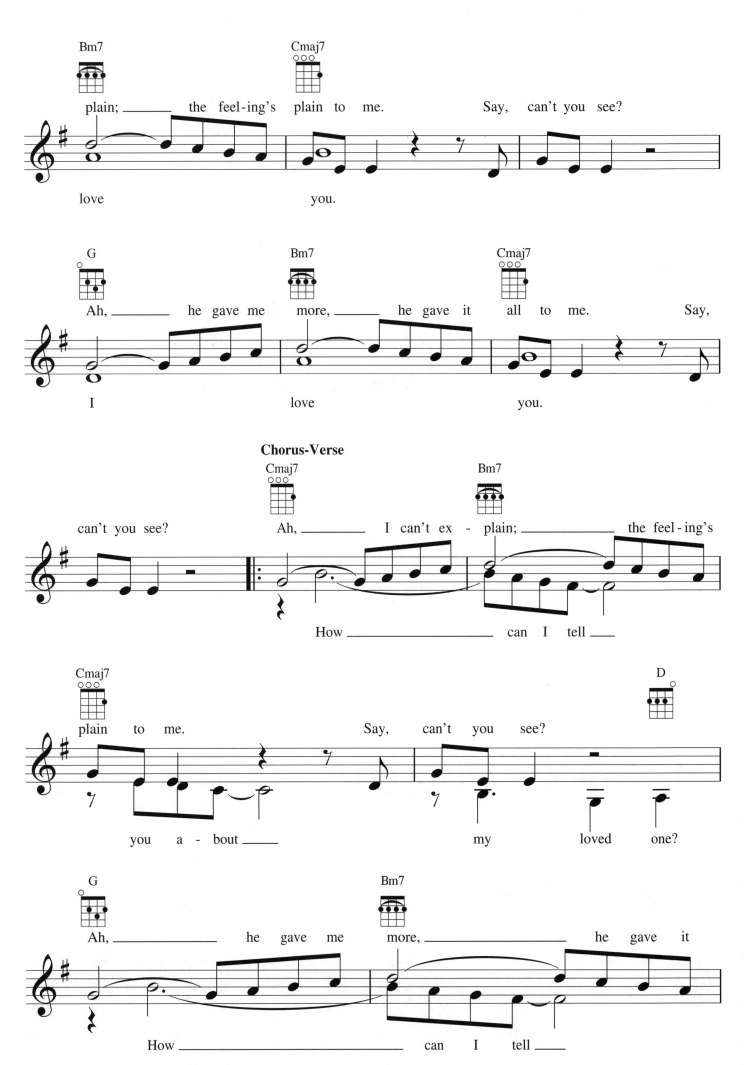

Outro-Verse

You'd think that peo - ple would have had e - nough of sil - ly love _ songs,

but I look a - round me and I see _____ it is - n't so. Oh, no. _____

Some peo - ple wan - na fill the world _____ with sil - ly love songs,

and what's wrong with that? _____

Sister Golden Hair

Words and Music by Gerry Beckley

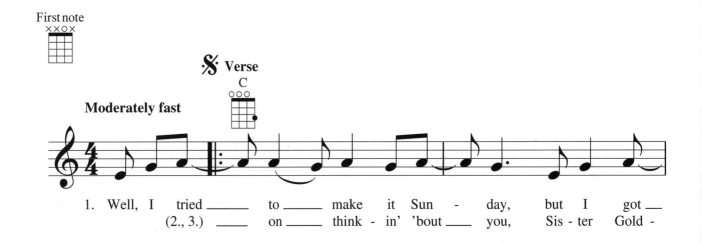

1. Well, I tried _____ to _____ make it Sun - day, but I got _____
(2., 3.) _____ on _____ think - in' 'bout _____ you, Sis - ter Gold -

_____ so _____ damned de - pressed _____ that I set _____
- en _____ Hair sur - prise, _____ and I just _____

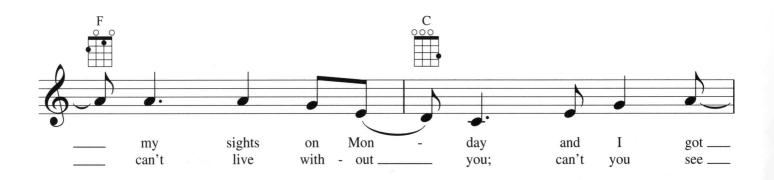

_____ my sights on Mon - day and I got _____
_____ can't live with - out _____ you; can't you see _____

_____ my - self _____ un - dressed. _____ I ain't read - y for the al -
_____ it in _____ my eyes? _____ I been one _____ poor cor - re - spond -

-tar,   but I   do _____ a - gree _____ there's _ times _
-ent,   and I been too, _____ too hard _ to _____ find, _

_____   when a wom - an   sure _____ can be _
_____   but it does - n't   mean _____ you ain't _

_____ a friend _ of mine.
_____ been on _____ my mind.

2. Well, I keep _

Chorus

Will you _ meet _____ me   in the mid - dle?   Will you _ meet _

_____ me in the air? _____   Will you love _____ me just a lit -

- tle,   just e - nough _____ to   show you care? _

197

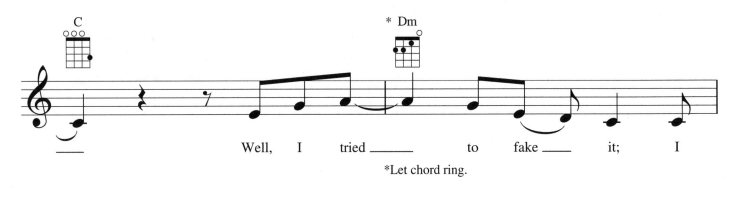

Well, I tried ____ to fake ____ it; I

*Let chord ring.

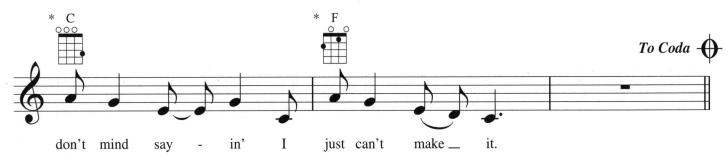

don't mind say - in' I just can't make __ it.

Interlude

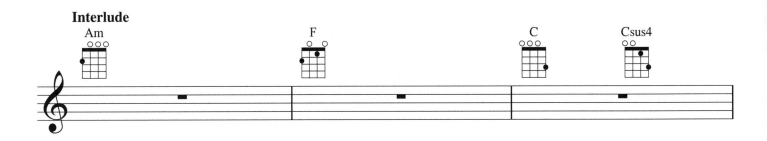

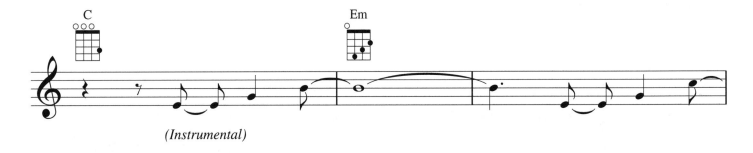

(Instrumental)

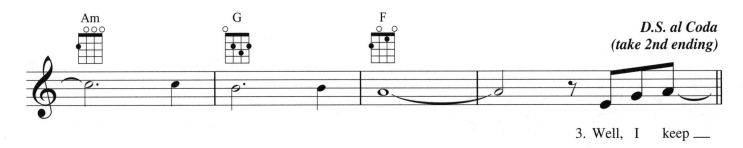

D.S. al Coda
(take 2nd ending)

3. Well, I keep __

Coda

Outro

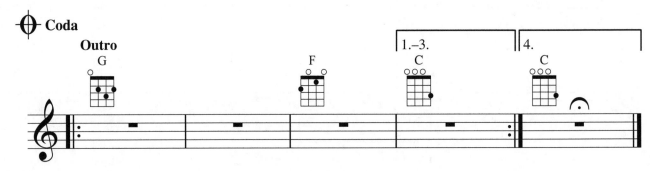

Three Times a Lady

Words and Music by Lionel Richie

and I love _____ you. _____ Yes, you're once, ___

___ twice, ___ three times ___ a la - dy,

and I love _____ you. _____

I love _____ you. _____

Verse

2. When we are to - geth - er, the

mo - ments I cher - ish ___ with ev - 'ry beat ___ of my ___

Snowbird

Words and Music by Gene MacLellan

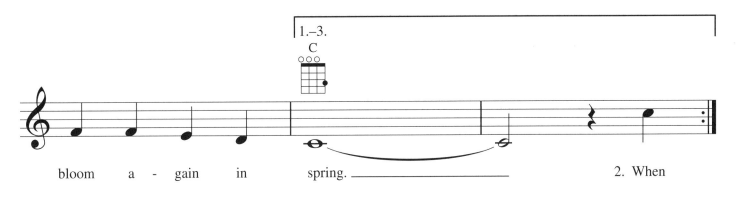

bloom a - gain in spring. _____ 2. When

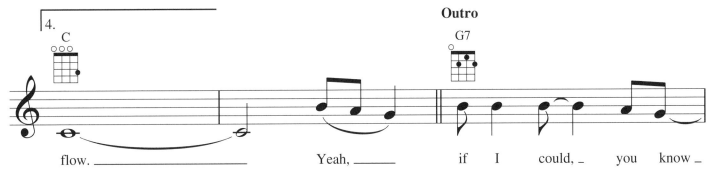

flow. _____ Yeah, _____ if I could, _ you know _

Outro

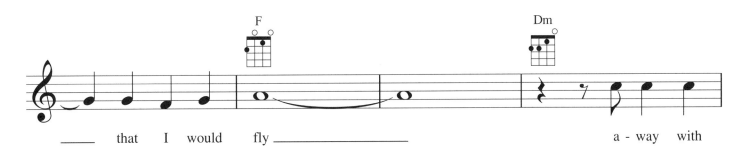

_____ that I would fly _____ a - way with

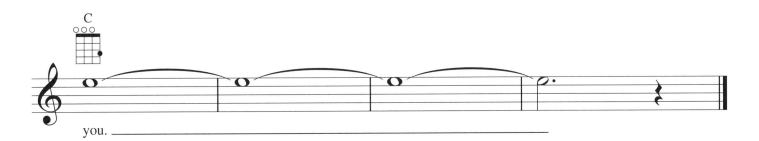

you. _____

Additional Lyrics

2. When I was young my heart was young then, too,
   And anything that it would tell me, that's the thing that I would do.
   But now I feel such emptiness within,
   For the thing I want the most in life the is thing that I can't win.

3. Spread your tiny wings and fly away,
   And take the snow back with you where it came from on that day.
   The one I love forever is untrue,
   And if I could, you know that I would fly away with you.

4. The breeze along the river seems to say
   That he'll only break my heart again should I decide to stay.
   So, little snowbird, take me with you when you go
   To that land of gentle breezes where the peaceful waters flow.

Sundown

Words and Music by Gordon Lightfoot

Additional Lyrics

2. She's been looking like a queen in a sailor's dream,
   And she don't always say what she really means.
   Sometimes I think it's a shame when I get feeling better when I'm feeling no pain.
   Sometimes I think it's a shame when I get feeling better when I'm feeling no pain.

3. I can picture ev'ry move that a man could make.
   Getting lost in her loving is your first mistake.
   Sundown, you better take care if I find you been creepin' 'round my back stairs.
   Sometimes I think it's a sin when I feel like I'm winning when I'm losing again.

4. I can see her looking fast in her faded jeans.
   She's a hard-loving woman, got me feeling mean.
   Sometimes I think it's a shame when I get feeling better when I'm feeling no pain.
   Sundown, you better take care if I find you been creepin' 'round my back stairs.

Sweet Home Alabama

Words and Music by Ronnie Van Zant, Ed King and Gary Rossington

1. Big wheels, keep on turn-ing, car-ry me home to see my
2. *See additional lyrics*

kin.

Sing-ing songs a-bout the South-land,

I miss ol' 'Bam-y once a-gain. __ *(And I think it's a sin.)* Sweet home Al-a-

bam-a, where the skies are so blue,

sweet home Al-a-bam-a, Lord, I'm com-ing home to

Additional Lyrics

3. Well, I heard Mr. Young sing about her.
   Well, I heard ol' Neil put her down.
   Well, I hope Neil Young will remember
   A southern man don't need him around anyhow.

4. Now, Muscle Shoals has got the Swampers,
   And they've been known to pick a tune or two.
   Lord, they get me off so much.
   They pick me up when I'm feeling blue.
   (Now, how 'bout you?)

We've Only Just Begun

Words and Music by Roger Nichols and Paul Williams

1. We've on-ly just be-gun _____ to live. _____
_____ White lace and prom - is - es, a kiss for luck _____ and we're on our way. _____

2. Be - fore the ris - ing
3., 4. And when the eve - ning

sun, _____ we fly. _____
comes, _____ we smile. _____

So man-y roads to choose;
So much of life a - head;

we start out walk - ing and learn to run. _____
we'll find a place _____ where there's room to grow. _____

To Coda

When I Need You

Words and Music by Carole Bayer Sager and Albert Hammond

The Wreck of the Edmund Fitzgerald

Words and Music by Gordon Lightfoot

1. The leg - end lives _ on ____ from the Chip - pe - wa on
2.–14. *See additional lyrics*

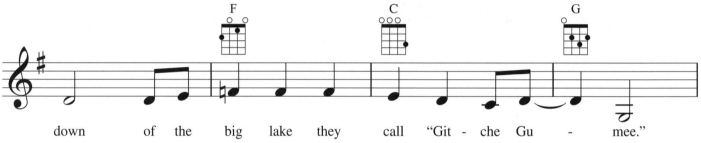

down of the big lake they call "Git - che Gu - mee."

The lake, it is ___ said, ___

____ nev - er ___ gives up her dead ___ when the skies ___ of No -

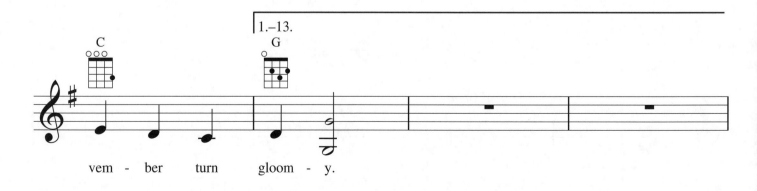

1.–13.

vem - ber turn gloom - y.

Outro

2. With a ear - ly."

(Instrumental)

Repeat and fade

Additional Lyrics

2. With a load of iron ore twenty-six thousand tons more
   Than the Edmund Fitzgerald weighed empty,
   That good ship and true was a bone to be chewed
   When the gales of November came early.

3. The ship was the pride of the American side
   Coming back from some mill in Wisconsin.
   As the big freighters go, it was bigger than most,
   With a crew and a captain well seasoned.

(continued on next page)

4. Concluding some terms with a couple of steel firms
   When they left fully loaded for Cleveland.
   And later that night when the ship's bell rang,
   Could it be the north wind they'd been feelin'?

5. The wind in the wires made a tattletale sound
   And a wave broke over the railing.
   And ev'ry man knew, as the captain did too,
   'Twas the witch of November come stealin'.

6. The dawn came late and the breakfast had to wait
   When the gales of November came slashin'.
   When afternoon came, it was freezin' rain
   In the face of a hurricane west wind.

7. When suppertime came, the old cook came on deck
   Sayin', "Fellas, it's too rough to feed ya."
   At seven p.m. a main hatchway caved in.
   He said, "Fellas, it's been good to know ya!"

8. The captain wired in he had water comin' in
   And the good ship and crew was in peril.
   And later that night when his lights went outta sight
   Came the wreck of the Edmund Fitzgerald.

9. Does anyone know where the love of God goes
   When the waves turn the minutes to hours?
   The searchers all say they'd have made Whitefish Bay
   If they'd put fifteen more miles behind her.

10. They might have split up or they might have capsized.
    They may have broke deep and took water.
    And all that remains is the faces and the names
    Of the wives and the sons and the daughters.

11. Lake Huron rolls, Superior sings
    In the rooms of her ice-water mansion.
    Old Michigan steams like a young man's dreams;
    The islands and bays are for sportsmen.

12. And farther below, Lake Ontario
    Takes in what Lake Erie can send her.
    And the iron boats go, as the mariners all know,
    With the gales of November remembered.

13. In a musty old hall in Detroit they prayed
    In the Maritime Sailors' Cathedral.
    The church bell chimed till it rang twenty-nine times
    For each man on the Edmund Fitzgerald.

14. The legend lives on from the Chippewa on down
    Of the big lake they call "Gitche Gumee."
    "Superior," they said, "never gives up her dead
    When the gales of November come early."

Why Don't We Get Drunk

Words and Music by Jimmy Buffett

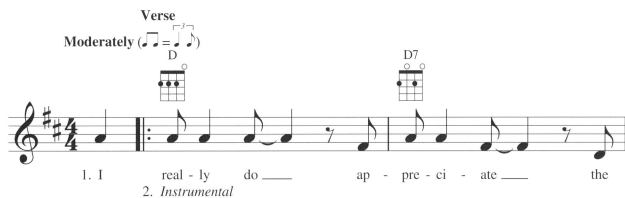

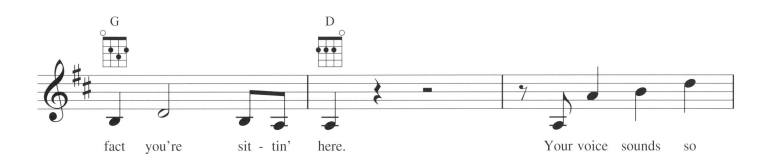

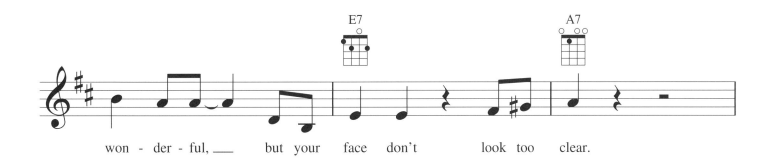

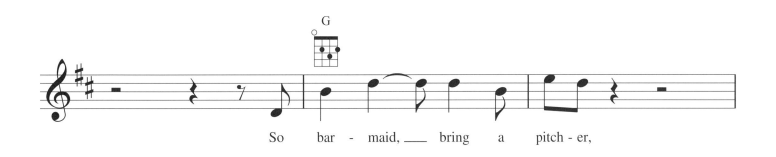

an - oth - er round — of brew. ____ Hon - ey,

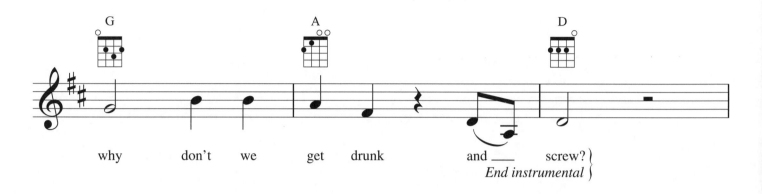

why don't we get drunk and — screw?
End instrumental

Chorus

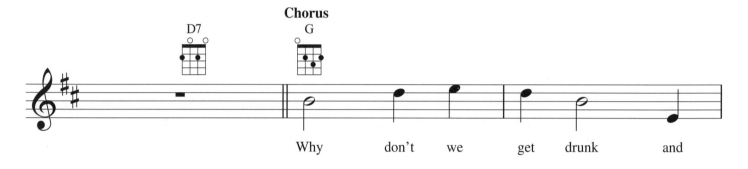

Why don't we get drunk and

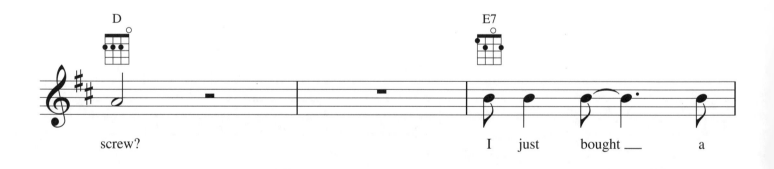

screw? I just bought — a

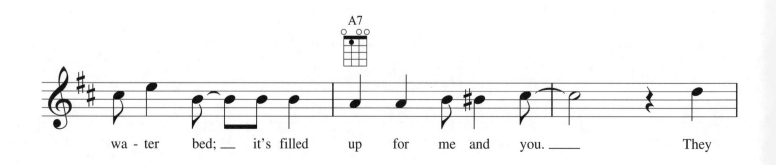

wa - ter bed; — it's filled up for me and you. ____ They

216

say you are a snuff ____ queen. Hon - ey,

I don't think ___ that's _ true. ____ So why don't we

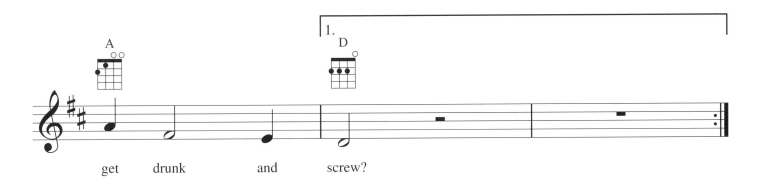

get drunk and screw?

screw? Yeah, _ now, ba - by, I ___ said, why don't we

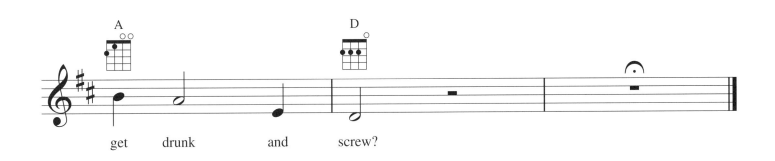

get drunk and screw?

Yesterday Once More

Words and Music by John Bettis and Richard Carpenter

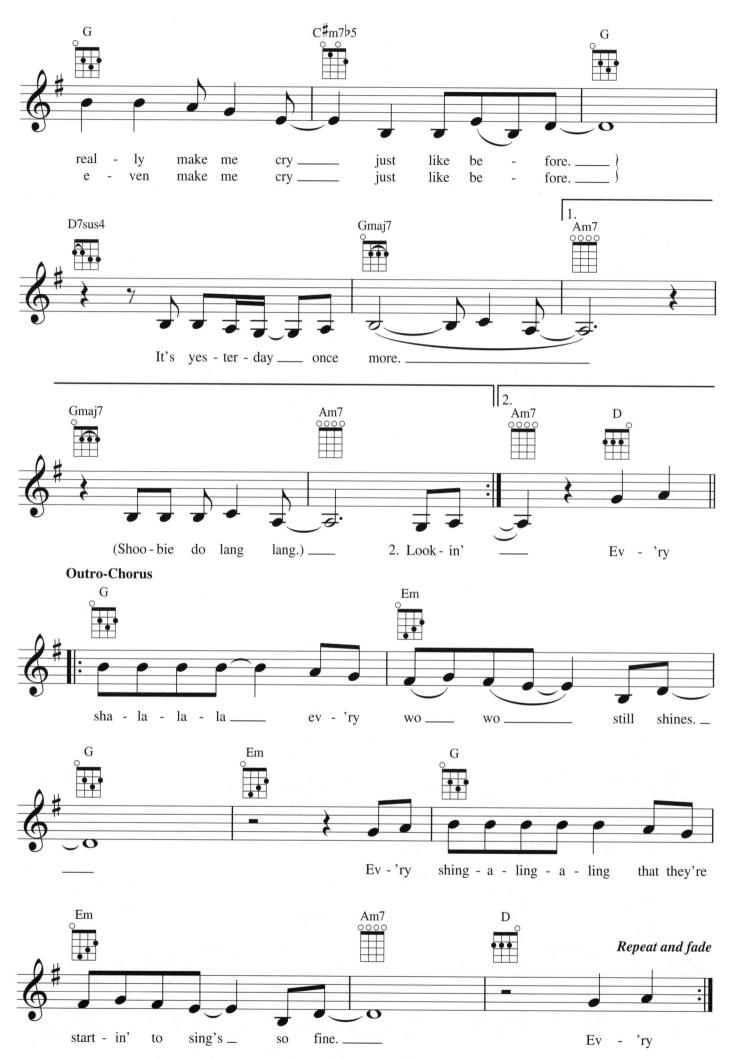

Y.M.C.A.

Words and Music by Jacques Morali, Henri Belolo and Victor Willis

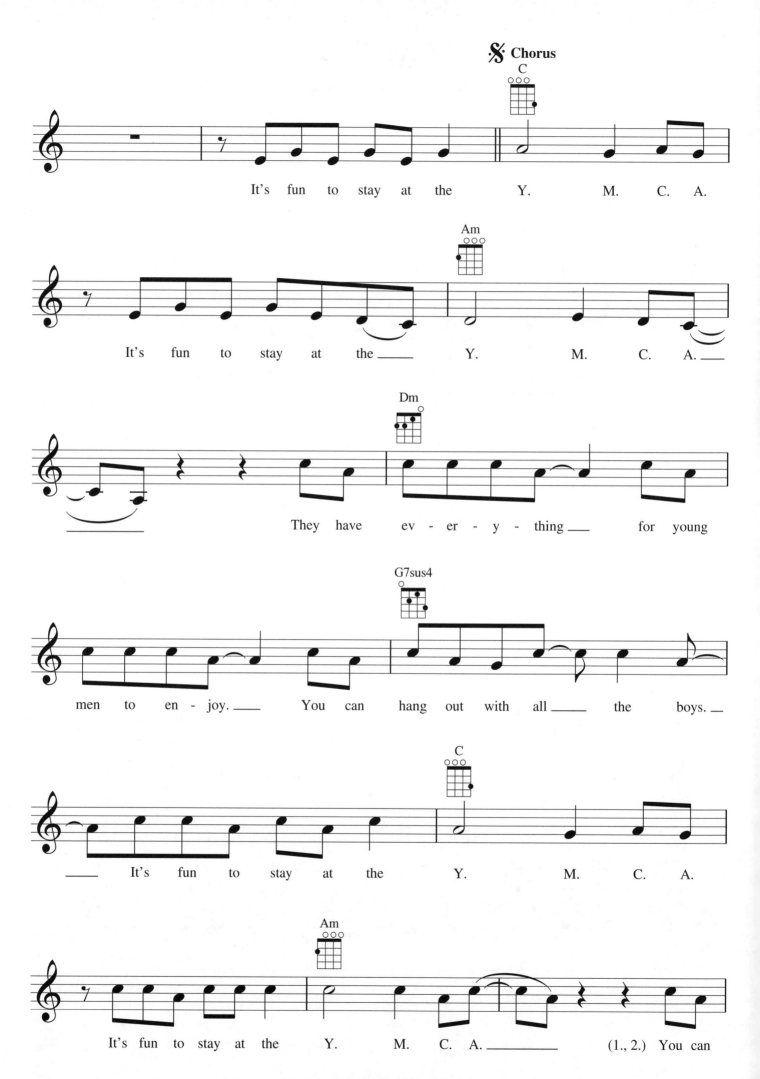

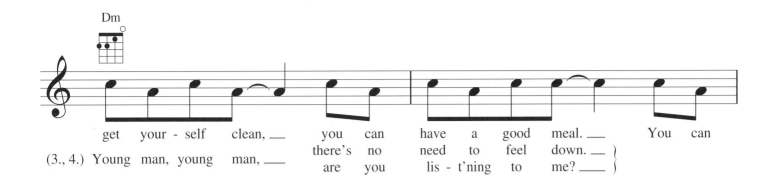

get your-self clean, ___ you can have a good meal. ___ You can
(3., 4.) Young man, young man, ___ there's no need to feel down. ___)
are you lis - t'ning to me? ___)

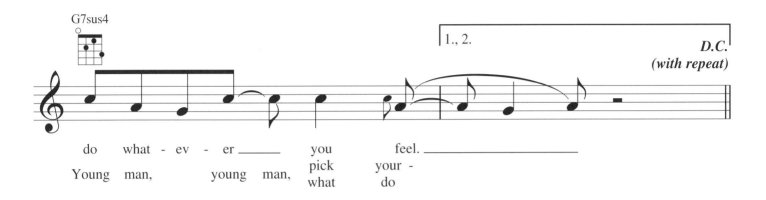

1., 2.

D.C.
(with repeat)

do what - ev - er ___ you feel. _____
Young man, young man, pick your -
what do

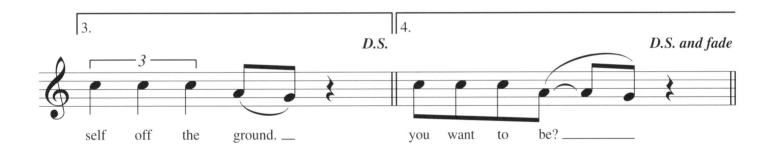

3.

D.S.

4.

D.S. and fade

self off the ground. ___ you want to be? ___

Additional Lyrics

3. Young man, are you listening to me?
   I said, young man, what do you want to be?
   I said, young man, you can make real your dreams
   But you've got to know this one thing:

4. No man does it all by himself.
   I said, young man, put your pride on the shelf
   And just go there to the Y.M.C.A.
   I'm sure they can help you today.

5. Young man, I was once in your shoes.
   I said, I was down and out and with the blues.
   I felt no man cared if I were alive.
   I felt the whole world was so jive.

6. That's when someone came up to me
   And said, "Young man, take a walk up the street.
   It's a place there called the Y.M.C.A.
   They can start you back on your way."

You Are So Beautiful

Words and Music by Billy Preston and Bruce Fisher

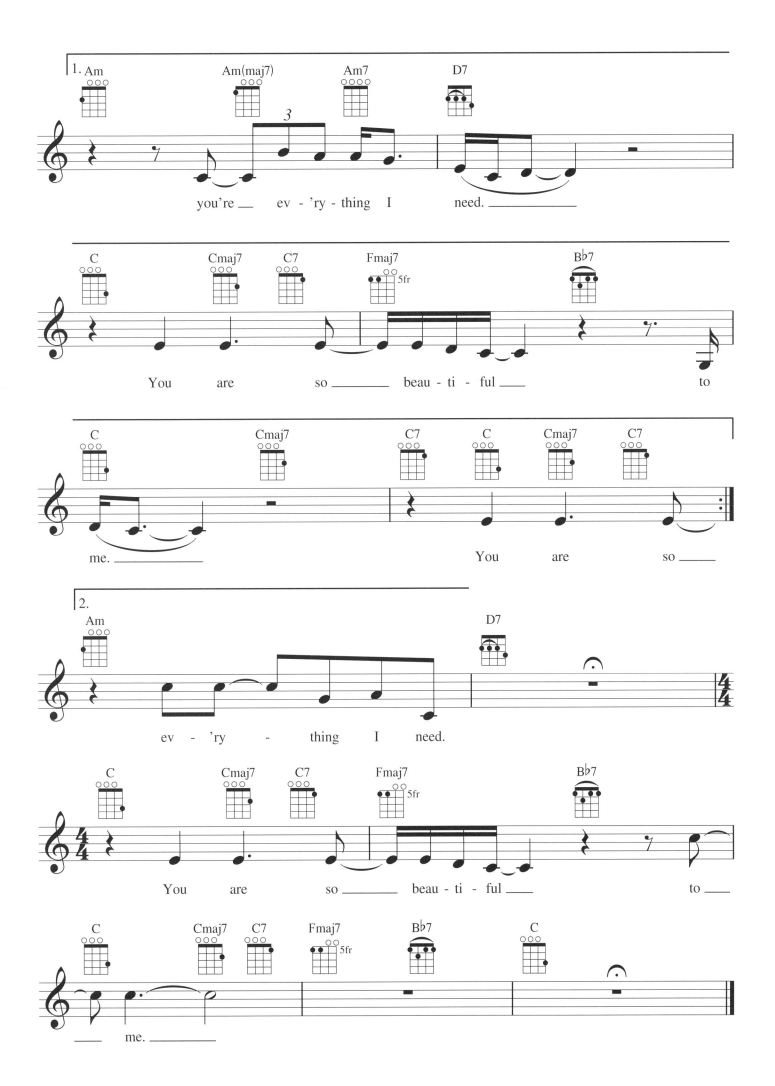

You Make Me Feel Like Dancing

Words and Music by Vini Poncia and Leo Sayer

Chorus

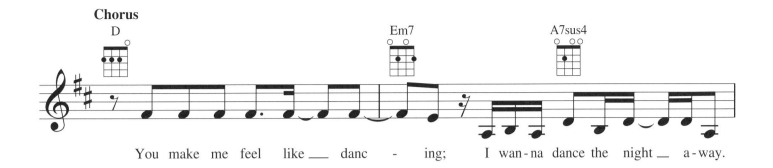

You make me feel like ___ danc - ing; I wan-na dance the night ___ a-way.

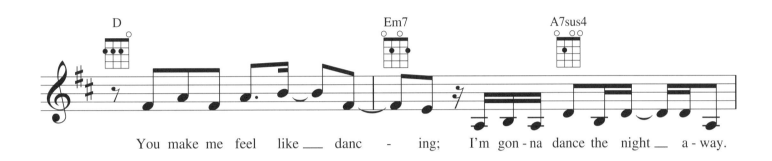

You make me feel like ___ danc - ing; I'm gon-na dance the night ___ a-way.

You make me feel like ___ danc - ing. I feel ___ like

danc - ing, ___ (woo!) danc - ing, ___ (woo!) dance the night ___ a - way. I feel like

danc - ing, ___ (woo!) danc - ing, ___ ah. ___

Interlude

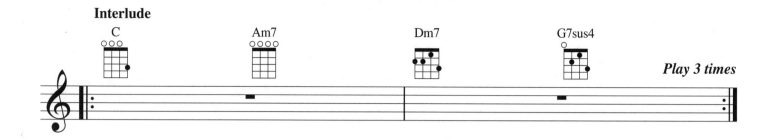

Play 3 times

Pre-Chorus

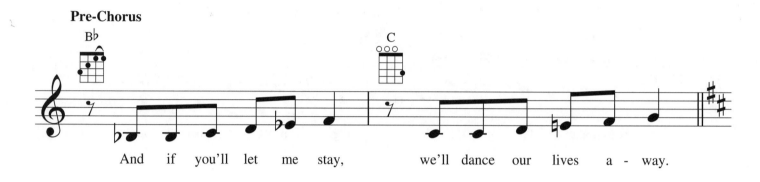

And if you'll let me stay, we'll dance our lives a - way.

Outro-Chorus

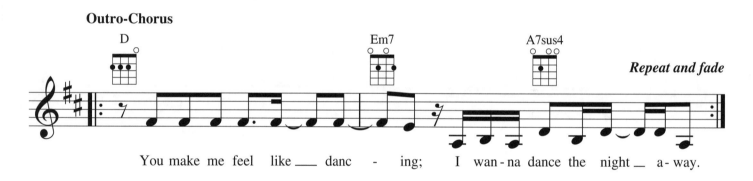

Repeat and fade

You make me feel like __ danc - ing; I wan - na dance the night __ a - way.

Additional Lyrics

2. Quarter to four in the morning,
   I ain't feeling tired, no, no, no.
   Just hold me tight and leave on the light
   'Cause I don't wanna go home.
   You put a spell on me;
   I'm right where you want me to be.

You've Got a Friend

Words and Music by Carole King

Additional Lyrics

2. If the sky above you should turn dark and full of clouds
   And that old North wind should begin to blow,
   Keep your head together and call my name out loud, now.
   Soon I'll be knockin' upon your door.

Your Mama Don't Dance

Words and Music by Jim Messina and Kenny Loggins

find   a   place to park.   You   hop in - to   the   back   seat where you

know it's nice and dark. __   You're   just a - bout   to   move   and you're

think - ing it's a breeze, __   there's a   light in your eye and then a guy ___ says,

"Out of the car, long hair!" Ooh - whee! ___   "You're com - ing with

me!"   The lo - cal po - lice!   And it's all be - cause your

Outro-Chorus

ma - ma don't dance   and your   dad - dy don't rock   and roll. __

Your ma - ma don't dance and your

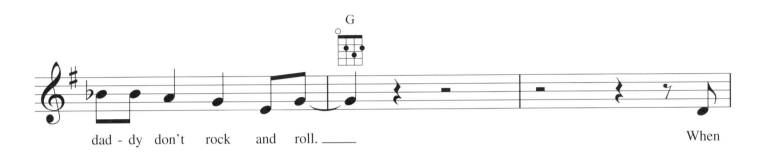

dad - dy don't rock and roll. _____ When

eve - ning rolls a - round and it's time to go to town, __ where do you

go to rock and roll? Where do you

go to rock and roll? Where do you

go to rock and roll?

You Needed Me

Words and Music by Randy Goodrum

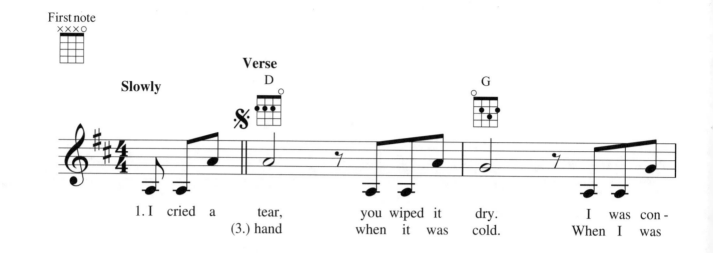

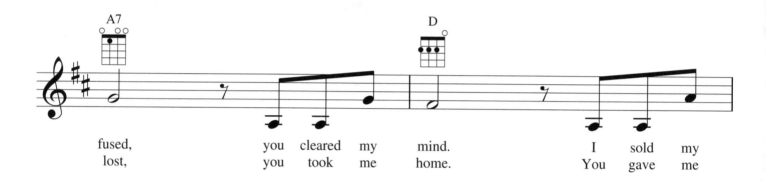

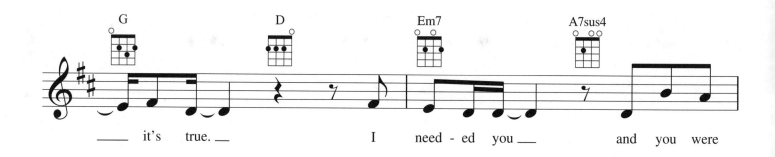

_____ it's true. _____ I need-ed you _____ and you were

there. _ And I'll nev-er leave; _ why should _ I leave? _ I'd be _

_____ a fool, _____ 'cause I've fi-n'lly found _ some-one _ who real - ly cares. _

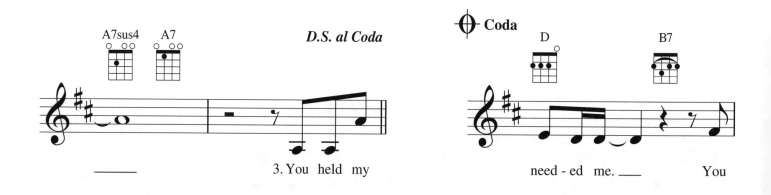

D.S. al Coda

Coda

_____ 3. You held my need-ed me. _____ You

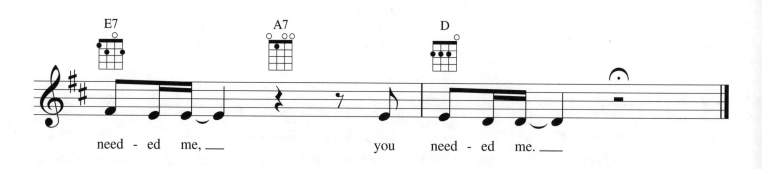

need-ed me, _____ you need-ed me. _____

Ride the Ukulele Wave!

The Beach Boys for Ukulele

This folio features 20 favorites, including: Barbara Ann • Be True to Your School • California Girls • Fun, Fun, Fun • God Only Knows • Good Vibrations • Help Me Rhonda • I Get Around • In My Room • Kokomo • Little Deuce Coupe • Sloop John B • Surfin' U.S.A. • Wouldn't It Be Nice • and more!

00701726 . . . . $14.99

The Beatles for Ukulele

Ukulele players can strum, sing and pick along with 20 Beatles classics! Includes: All You Need Is Love • Eight Days a Week • Good Day Sunshine • Here, There and Everywhere • Let It Be • Love Me Do • Penny Lane • Yesterday • and more.

00700154 . . . . $16.99

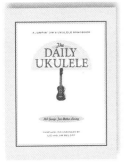

The Daily Ukulele

compiled and arranged by Liz and Jim Beloff
Strum a different song everyday with easy arrangements of 365 of your favorite songs in one big songbook! Includes favorites by the Beatles, Beach Boys, and Bob Dylan, folk songs, pop songs, kids' songs, Christmas carols, and Broadway and Hollywood tunes, all with a spiral binding for ease of use.

00240356 . . . . $34.99

The Daily Ukulele – Leap Year Edition

366 More Songs for Better Living
compiled and arranged by Liz and Jim Beloff
An amazing second volume with 366 MORE songs for you to master each day of a leap year! Includes: Ain't No Sunshine • Calendar Girl • I Got You Babe • Lean on Me • Moondance • and many, many more.

00240681 . . . . $34.99

Disney Songs for Ukulele

20 great Disney classics arranged for all uke players, including: Beauty and the Beast • Bibbidi-Bobbidi-Boo (The Magic Song) • Can You Feel the Love Tonight • Chim Chim Cher-ee • Heigh-Ho • It's a Small World • Some Day My Prince Will Come • We're All in This Together • When You Wish upon a Star • and more.

00701708 . . . . $12.99

Folk Songs for Ukulele

A great collection to take along to the campfire! 60 folk songs, including: Amazing Grace • Buffalo Gals • Camptown Races • For He's a Jolly Good Fellow • Good Night Ladies • Home on the Range • I've Been Working on the Railroad • Kumbaya • My Bonnie Lies over the Ocean • On Top of Old Smoky • Scarborough Fair • Swing Low, Sweet Chariot • Take Me Out to the Ball Game • Yankee Doodle • and more.

00696068 . . . . $12.99

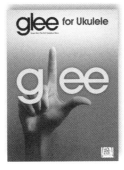

Glee

Music from the Fox Television Show for Ukulele
20 favorites for Gleeks to strum and sing, including: Bad Romance • Beautiful • Defying Gravity • Don't Stop Believin' • No Air • Proud Mary • Rehab • True Colors • and more.

00701722 . . . . $14.99

Hawaiian Songs for Ukulele

Over thirty songs from the state that made the ukulele famous, including: Beyond the Rainbow • Hanalei Moon • Ka-lu-a • Lovely Hula Girl • Mele Kalikimaka • One More Aloha • Sea Breeze • Tiny Bubbles • Waikiki • and more.

00696065 . . . . $9.99

Jack Johnson – Strum & Sing

Cherry Lane Music
Strum along with 41 Jack Johnson songs using this top-notch collection of chords and lyrics just for the uke! Includes: Better Together • Bubble Toes • Cocoon • Do You Remember • Flake • Fortunate Fool • Good People • Holes to Heaven • Taylor • Tomorrow Morning • and more.

02501702 . . . . $10.99

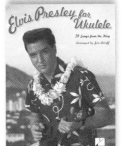

Elvis Presley for Ukulele

arr. Jim Beloff
20 classic hits from The King: All Shook Up • Blue Hawaii • Blue Suede Shoes • Can't Help Falling in Love • Don't • Heartbreak Hotel • Hound Dog • Jailhouse Rock • Love Me • Love Me Tender • Return to Sender • Suspicious Minds • Teddy Bear • and more.

00701004 . . . . $14.99

Jake Shimabukuro – Peace Love Ukulele

Deemed "the Hendrix of the ukulele," Hawaii native Jake Shimabukuro is a uke virtuoso. Our songbook features note-for-note transcriptions with ukulele tablature of Jake's masterful playing on all the CD tracks: Bohemian Rhapsody • Boy Meets Girl • Bring Your Adz • Hallelujah • Pianoforte 2010 • Variation on a Dance 2010 • and more, plus two bonus selections!

00702516 . . . . $19.99

Worship Songs for Ukulele

25 worship songs: Amazing Grace (My Chains are Gone) • Blessed Be Your Name • Enough • God of Wonders • Holy Is the Lord • How Great Is Our God • In Christ Alone • Love the Lord • Mighty to Save • Sing to the King • Step by Step • We Fall Down • and more.

00702546 . . . . $12.99

HAL•LEONARD® CORPORATION

7777 W. Bluemound Rd. P.O. Box 13819 Milwaukee, WI 53213

Prices, contents, and availability subject to change.

0913

Now you can play your favorite songs on your uke with great-sounding backing tracks to help you sound like a bona fide pro! This series includes the Amazing Slow Downer, so you can adjust the tempo without changing the pitch.

1. POP HITS
00701451 Book/CD Pack $14.99

2. UKE CLASSICS
00701452 Book/CD Pack $12.99

3. HAWAIIAN FAVORITES
00701453 Book/CD Pack $12.99

4. CHILDREN'S SONGS
00701454 Book/CD Pack $12.99

5. CHRISTMAS SONGS
00701696 Book/CD Pack $12.99

6. LENNON & MCCARTNEY
00701723 Book/CD Pack $12.99

7. DISNEY FAVORITES
00701724 Book/CD Pack $12.99

8. CHART HITS
00701745 Book/CD Pack $14.99

9. THE SOUND OF MUSIC
00701784 Book/CD Pack $12.99

10. MOTOWN
00701964 Book/CD Pack $12.99

11. CHRISTMAS STRUMMING
00702458 Book/CD Pack $12.99

12. BLUEGRASS FAVORITES
00702584 Book/CD Pack $12.99

13. UKULELE SONGS
00702599 Book/CD Pack $12.99

14. JOHNNY CASH
00702615 Book/CD Pack $14.99

15. COUNTRY CLASSICS
00702834 Book/CD Pack $12.99

16. STANDARDS
00702835 Book/CD Pack $12.99

17. POP STANDARDS
00702836 Book/CD Pack $12.99

18. IRISH SONGS
00703086 Book/CD Pack $12.99

19. BLUES STANDARDS
00703087 Book/CD Pack $12.99

20. FOLK POP ROCK
00703088 Book/CD Pack $12.99

21. HAWAIIAN CLASSICS
00703097 Book/CD Pack $12.99

22. ISLAND SONGS
00703098 Book/CD Pack $12.99

23. TAYLOR SWIFT
00704106 Book/CD Pack $14.99

24. WINTER WONDERLAND
00101871 Book/CD Pack $12.99

25. GREEN DAY
00110398 Book/CD Pack $14.99

HAL•LEONARD® CORPORATION

7777 W. BLUEMOUND RD. P.O. BOX 13819 MILWAUKEE, WI 53213

www.halleonard.com

Prices, contents, and availability subject to change without notice.

0913